ICE BLACK BLACK ICE

Chandochitemachiororopagomo

Innocent B. (Hondo) Chirawu

authorHOUSE®

AuthorHouse™ UK
1663 Liberty Drive
Bloomington, IN 47403 USA
www.authorhouse.co.uk
Phone: 0800.197.4150

Published by AuthorHouse 11/21/2018

ISBN: 978-1-7283-8034-6 (sc)
ISBN: 978-1-7283-8033-9 (e)

What life has taught me
I would like to share

And until that day, the African continent
Will not know peace, we Africans will fight
We find it necessary and we know we shall win
As we are confident in the victory

Of good over evil, good over evil, good over evil
Good over evil, good over evil, good over evil

Bob Marley

WORDS OF WISDOM

(1) When one knocks on a door, they usually tap three (3) times (tap, tap, tap) with their knuckles while their fingers would be pointing at them. Can't that be a reminder there is only one Triune God whom them too should worship!

(2) Wherever one goes on this earth, there is only ONE sun and sometimes the world is referred to as a place "under the sun". Can't this be a reminder to all men that there is only ONE universal Son of God in whom we should place our faith for our spiritual enlightenment!

(3) Isn't it a true fact that it's easier to elevate the lowly or humble because they leave enough room above their heads for that to happen without any hassles!

(4) Isn't it True that:

a) Failure to Plan is Planning to Fail;

b) In success there is a degree of failure but more still in failure lies is a great deal success (someone may have failed a thousand times before they succeeded in their invention);

c) If one doesn't Stand for Something they are most likely to Fall for Anything (If one aims at the moon they might catch a star);

d) One who spends more time on his knees cannot fall because he is already on the ground;

5) Isn't it a common statement that 'seeing is believing' and yet because our physical eyes have limited vision, they is so much they can't see and yet so true – to start with they can't even on their own see themselves with themselves".

INTRODUCTION

A United States of Africa is not a mirage or a utopia but practical reality in the making. Having been born and bred in "apartheid Rhodesia" where Mudi a.k.a. Ice Black lost his whole childhood, Mudi loves the Economic Freedom Forum.

By rallying behind a revolutionary party like the EFF I believe Africans can realise then dream, Yes, We can as long as we remember that United we Stand, Divided we Fall. Once more we will be like them that dream, when look back at the 1884 Imperialist disaster which partitioned the mother of continent into assorted sad colonial allotments. Africa Woye, Viva Our Revolutionaries, Viva Kwame Nkrumah, Viva Haile Sellasie, Viva Jomo Kenyatta, Viva Kenneth Kaunda, Viva Julius K. Nyerere, Viva Samora Machel, Viva Maummar Gaddaffi, Viva Thomas Sankala, Viva Steve Biko, Viva Nelson Mandela, Viva Robert Mugabe (for saying among other things to the West "Keep your money and we take back our land.........show me one black African who owns land or a farm in England and I will give back the farms I took ….."), to name a few Viva Africa. Africa will NEVER be colonised again!!! Honestly, I Look forward with an outstretched neck for that day when South Africa will be called by its revolutionary name Azania and together with other African states constitute the new USA (United States of Africa) practically enjoying full ownership and control of her natural resources (especially land and all that comes with it, for example wildlife and minerals thereof, the aqua world within their space and everything within the entire space above them), own their production and means of production, determine and dictate the price of their resources and products, for example gold, diamonds and oil, having a one common central bank, one common currency valued on the strength of her own gold bar resources, one president and speaking one language kiSwahili. It is then and only then that mother Africa, the cradle of civilization that bears the umbrical cord of the earth can without shame or apology, with her chin up and shoulders square boldy say she has regained her unadulterated originality, true Uhuru and Umoja as a Nation. One Africa, One Nation! United States of Africa Woye! Forward with the Revolution! Aluta continua until we complete the Revolution! Victory is Certain!

CHAPTER 1

Mudi's says there are a Dozen Questions which many people of ethnic minority backgrounds in diasporas dare not ask probably because the answers thereof are obvious and the so-called First World systems have a common way of dealing with the obvious answer – they simply "give a blind eye or sweep under the carpet, threaten and frustrate the victim(s)":

Question 1: Why is there No Black Stripe in the Union Jack, when a lot of black people died for instance in Burma defending the English Queen of the day and her commonwealth interests.

Question 2: Why is the 10thMonth the only month of the 12 calendar months marked The Black History month, whose story is being celebrated in the rest 11 months of the year?

Question 3: Why is the black man expected to work 100 times more to be considered "good or satisfactory"? That's what Mudi was told by a Filipino mentor who bootlicked a caucasian ward manager who never called Mudi by name but wearing "a perhaps" on her lips always went "young man" when Mudi was on his 2nd nurse training placement and his then university of nuffinghi in lucrative business with Malais and Shanghi did nuffing about it except saying after 3 months "Your mentor will be able to sign you now because the former manager she was afraid of was promoted to head a neighbouring ward. What? "Promoted?" my foot!

Question 4: Whyshould "I and I" a black man expected to pronounce English words and English names properly far much more than my white counterpart is required to concerning non-English or ethnic minority words and names?

Question 5: Why is there no proportional racial representation in most institutions in the UK and the rest of the so-called 1st World countries, and more specifically within professional positions like Fire Brigade Chief Marshals, School Headteachers, University Vice Chancellors, Her Majesty's Guards, Media executives, Right Wing or Left Wing political leaders, army chiefs, police chiefs and Parliamentarians with special posts without even mentioning Speaker of parliament –are people of my complexion too dark to be noticed for proportional inclusion and promotion?

Question 6: Why are ethnic minority children especially those of Afro-Carribean backgrounds more likely to be excluded from school than their white counterparts/peers?

Question 7: Why are there hardly any individuals of black, Afro-Carribean or ethnic minority who own land or farms in the UK and mostof the so called 1st World countries

Question 8: Why does the general public opinion perceive or hold the common view that chances of a black premier in the UK are next to nil, like what some of my former students expressed "No Chance!" after I expressed my dream of becoming a British prime minister in future.

Question 9: Why is the general ratio of interracial marriages skewed or tilted more towards black men marrying white women than white men marrying black women?

Question 10: Why is Racism a subject avoided as much as possible, many a time swept under the carpet and often the complainant or victim required to prove 100% or beyond any doubt that their claim is true, especially when the victim is black of belongs to the ethnic minority background.

Question 11: (a) Why are there so many double standards in the UK and most of the so-called 1ˢᵗ World societies, civil policies e.g. subtle xenophobia towards foreigners, especially towards blacks forgetting that what goes around comes around and the "Disrespect" which was started by their ancestors through enslavement of blacks is no exception especially when they further open the scars through sophisticated, well calculated and subtle institutional racism and racism in its other forms hiding it behind the banner s of "We Are an Equal Opportunity Employer" and "Building a More Tolerant Society"

(b) Why does the head of a monarchy whose country owns not even a single diamond or gold mine possess one of the biggest if not the biggest refined diamond on her crown – could be linked to the decades and decades of uninterrupted wealth amassing which was enjoyed by her empire and predecessors who stacked all the rest of it into a pot they called "The Commonwealth". …..and when the robbed nations demand all their wealth back they are told, "that's ridiculous, we can't give all of it back; maybe if you participate in our Commonwealth Games we may give you back a little at a time in the form of a gold medal only for whichever sport you win". Is alarming then, that some of the worst enemies of the West are those who were formerly close to the West: some good examples of such are late, others alive and labelled by the West as "dictators, rebels or terrorists"

Question 12: Why are there more blacks or people of ethnic minority background with English first and second names compared to the number of European or Caucasian with non-English first and second names especially

3

African names, yet I have met many black people especially Africans and Afro-Carribeans with English/European names. I am yet to come across even a single Caucasian with an African first name and surname, just as much I am yet to come across a single black man who caused any world war.

A Sequil to Mudi's dozen questions above:

1. Why is Mudi called referred to as "black" and yet he is actually brown and why is brown Mudi expected to work 100 times more than his pink Ian counterpart?

2. Why are some people treated as being more equal than others in a nation which claims to be democratic and fair

3. Why is Mudi's off spring with his pink partner referred to as "Mixed Race" and not "Grey" since the same labellers call Mudi "Black" and his partner "White".

4. Why had the Nobel peace prize for Madiba to be shared between him and De Clerk who represented the system which Mandela was fighting against even in all his 27 years behind bars.

5. Why is everything good associated with "white" and everything bad associated with "black" - white wedding, white Christmas, snow white, and controversially "White Maggots" as opposed to black ball in snooker, black listing, blackmail, black sheep, black book, black eye, black moon and controversially "Black Panther" . Is it alarming that uncle Bob was quoted as saying, he doesn't mind whatever black is associated with as long as he uses white toilet paper to wipe his bottom.

6. Why do some TV program advert ask viewers to donate the same amount for a pet: a dog, a donkeys or whatever and for a child suffering abroad?

A small piece of advice:

If one was forced at gun point, God forbid, to pick up either a pale devil or a dark devil, Ice Black would advise them to pick a dark devil because he says he has never seen a dark vampire at the cinemas, all vampires and maggots are pale, pale, pale.

CHAPTER 2

Rhyme

Ion
Like a lion in
Zion Ion Lion Zion
Take heed to my whisper
Stay safe by more than a whisker
Aspire to inspire before you expire
Africa says he who bites your ear is dear
Keep precious words of advice like a pearl
Not to sell but to preserve as treasure
And like a golden pear
Not for eating but for wear right on your right ear
Me thinks that's cool & not queer
As would be with proper wear

INTERESTING LEARNING CURVES FOR
MUDI CROWNED BY A HUGE ONE

Tendencies of Autistic people

1. Love control

2. Egocentric – either ALL of it or NONE at all

3. Blunt – don't care about the effect of their words or behaviour to others

4. Hate sarcasm/struggle taking a joke

5. Routine – they just love routine and hate change

6. Like those with personality disorder, they can neither be satisfied nor ever receive enough of anything of their interest, including attention

7. Can easily ditch friends, girlfriend/boyfriend, partner or spouse if the other person doesn't talk their interest

8. Perfectionist attitude – close to OCD syndrome and quick to judge and roast others over same behaviour or worse than theirs. Hence, it's not alarming that Mudi's 1st partner (Vongai) and afterwards his 2nd ex-partner (nicknamed "Matron") after his first marriage broke down in 2013, who belonged a certain organisation both showed most of the above characteristics of behaviour and to top it all the later was a real "Drama Queen" who resented dissent voice or being questioned, yet she loved roasting others. She also had a problem of not knowing that she does not know what she does not know.....and this was worsened by her pronounced weakness of seeing thing in black and white and her exposure to some men of the cloth's teachings which she misinterpreted "big time" . For example, some statements that Mudi recalls her saying are:

   a) "If you meet me in an elevator and ask me 'are you going down?', I can answer you I'm going to the ground' because if I say 'I'm going down, my whole life would begin to go down', so I can never say that

b) "You know, it is possible in this day and age to live up to a thousand years or more if you want and decide to.... it's possible if you exercise your faith" When Mudi asked her if she meant all the great man of God who didn't make it 1000 years in our dispensation had no enough faith? She said "Yes". At one point she asked Mudi "How many millimetres are in a centimentre?" "Ten" answered Mudi. "No, they are 100!" she protested. When Mudi stuck to his answer, she challenged him "Google it! The laptop is right in front of you, google it". Mudi said he wouldn't do that because he was sure of his answer. "Why are you stubborn like that, is it a hard task to just google it!"

c) When Mudi received a phone call from anyone even male friend, she'd listen to the chat and as soon as Mudi hangs up, she would lecturing Mudi on silly stupid trivial things of a matter of preference in expression. "When you said "...." you should have said "....".

What the heck of a controlling woman! No wonder why one day whle driving she said to her friend over the phone "I eventually got that man you know. He is right here with me. 'Yeah, by force, I got him....by force by fire'. That was Matron – Mudi didn't call that for nothing.

d) Being Mudi's former vicar, Matron had subtly stalked Mudi when his 1st marriage was on the rocks, pretending at some early stages that "she would never go out with Mudi", then with time did her best to manuevour, manipulate Mudi into going out with her and when Mudi felt prone to gross abuse in the future he told her that they couldn't continue the relationship but, just like Vongai who vowed and organised Mudi's expulsion from university after Mudi ended his relationship with her due to her complex personality, she also couldn't take it lying down and started use religious statements to both manipulate and intimidate Mudi to "hang on" in the relationship "No reverse!" she said "if you do God will hold this against you. I did not keep myself away from my ex-husband for 14 years to have a man touch my breast and not marry me". Mudi asked her "What if yiou had a daughter and say a serial killer touched her breast would you still force that man to marry your daughter?" And her answer was "Yes, that's my principle!". Now, Mudi's big mistake was from that moment onwards "budged to her dictatorship": he became like a sheep to the slaughter, all the way down to the right altar, and Matron financed almost everything. Then when they were now a couple she started to show more of her true colours like roasting Mudi over silly petty things, for example, she said that Vongai was going to hell for having cause Mudi's expulsion from varsity, she got so angry when now Mudi told her to avoid being judgemental that she went into the kitchen wetted her hands at the sink and sprinkled water in Mudi's eyes saying "What sort of person are you, you support bad people!"

e) For 5 reason Mudi decided he 'd never reunite with Matron once they split up, the reason included, matron wanted to cut him off from his children t the extent that Mudi's heart bled on day after bumping into one of his children in her college friends company at the traffic lights in town and the child had walked away in opposite direction trying to avoid him – the reason was when the child had asked for money to meet her Prom expenses, Matron had said "Text the child's mother to foot the bill and then we can reimburse her later on" and that was soon after Mudi and Matron had just had a flashy wedding. Matron had also said to Mudi "If you ever think you can divorce me and marry a 25-year old, God will not allow you, and time is not in your hands. Do you know I can poison you!?

f) Mudi had to eventually agreed with her to separate for a while and that when she returns from attending a conference somewhere she would proceed same day to her former house which she let out to a lodger. Mudi had had enough of her complex personality by then. Knowing her enough that she'd change her mind and refuse to go upon her return from conference Mudi changed his change the key to his Flat's front door. After opening door for her upon her return from conference, she blew her top over the change of key and said she'd changed her mind she wasn't going anymore.

She got so agitated that she threw her mobile phone at Mudi but missed and Mudi called police on her. She shouted at Mudi and Mudi had to go outside as he talked to the police who only came the following day after she had left

9. Once allowed one inch to abuse, bully or exploit the other individual they take a foot a yard or even a mile. When shown love, affection, kindness or empathy they become addicted and struggle when to stop exploiting the benefits. They can only temporarily stop when either blood instead of milk begins to ooze or when the cow they are milking drops dead. They are the champions of beating all the day light out of a faulty cash leaking ATM chunning out cash at every tap of a button – this they can unashamedly do with anybody willing to entertain or meet their financial requests from one amount to another in an unreasonable escalating pattern. Hence, it's not alarming that one of Mudi's 3rd ex-partner (M1 Sout) after his 2nd eight-month-old-marriage divorce was concluded in early 2017, for a while kept a profile on her social media saying something like, "….. Dish out kindness like confetti" when she herself was as mean as a greedy fat cat. She had started the relationship by initially refusing to accept Mudi's proposal then eventually said

"since we are entering a relationship you will be my shoulder to cry on, can I borrow £300, then hardly 2 weeks later "can you help me with £250 because the £300 I borrowed was not enough for the need I was facing", Mudi budged and gave her, then from thereafter during the approximately one and half years of their relationship she asked for different amounts of not less than £500 each month – sometimes£600, £750, £850 etc. Like someone who had it all up her sleeve in the last month of their relationship she milked Mudi financially almost like a pros who had been let loose into a bank vault: she asked her friend's family out and asked Mudi to pay approx. £250 including tax fare to and from the place, then soon after that on the very same day she asked Mudi to transfer £850 into her bank account for her to pay her utility bills (a claim she knew sounded important) and a day or 2 afterward this, she texted Mudi to lend her £500 from Mudi's £1k saving which she said she knew Mudi didn't want to touch being part of the money Mudi had started putting aside for their future plans. She promised she was going to give back that money to Mudi the following Friday when she got paid. That never happened. Instead when Mudi met her on that Friday she said she had no money to pay back the £500 and added that Mudi wouldn't be able to meet her financial needs like she had pointed out before that her daughter and one of her own friends had told her she needed marry a hubby millionaire or else she would have to dedicate her time into live-in work meaning she would meet Mudi say once in 3 months or even only twice a year. Mudi then expressed how she made him feel by saying what she said quoting to her Maya Angelou's words about people forgetting what one did, but never forgetting how one made them feel, which was one of M1 Sout's favourite sayings which she had put on her profile sometime before. Mudi then tried illustrate explain how much he was doing the best he could to meet M1 Sout's financial needs, how Mudi up-to-date had parted with around £10k counting from the time they started going out with each other – from the £300 she had borrowed at the start of the relationship, followed by the £250 she asked for and many other amounts in between including the £500 she had last borrowed and failed to repay that day. Oh, oh, oh at the mention of that all hell broke loose! She snapped charged at Mudi expressing her shock at the fact that Mudi dared mention that. "So, you were counting! Counting!!! That's it this relationship has to end. That's it. Finish." Then Mudi apologised profusely, kneeling next to her knees as she sat in her sofa. Mudi said he was doing his best and he felt like one losing an arm and a leg in his efforts to meet her financial needs. "I f I ask for your *hand* or leg be chopped for me, whats wrong with that…..wouldn't you let me have them!" she snapped. "But Honey, the way things are happening it seems we are not cutting our garment according to its size…..you wouldn't ask for my head as well, would you?" Mudi asked at which point she snapped "What would be wrong with that if I want your head?" Mudi the said "Honey, are you talking figuratively like I am talking or literally?" "Literally" she said as she stood up going to the kitchen "You can never understand it" After a few moments Mudi followed her to the kitchen. Looking into the kitchen sink she said, "Do you know that my late husband died for my sake". Mudi asked her what she meant by that but she said that Mudi wouldn't understand it.

It was only like a week later after M1 Sout had spewed or elbowed him out of her life that Mudi recalled how she had several times talked about her dream to own a Care home and that her late hubby wanted to buy her one. Unfortunately, the late hubby had got shot in the middle of a cash making oil deal. Adding two and two to get a four, it flashed in my mind that, the cash in question could have been earmarked for the Care Home project if the deal had succeeded. It also dawned in Mudi's mind that "partner" is the appropriate term M! Should probably use to refer to her late baby father, since according to her own words earlier the man was linked to 2 other women older than M1 Sout with whom he had older children before he impregnated M1 with a baby girl, living in with M1 for a while, split up and then after travelling here and there abroad would come and put up at M1's place, who now was like the younger concubine.

In Mudi's effort to impress M1 South, even though she had failed to give back the £500 she had borrowed the previous week on top of the approximately £1100 Mudi had parted with for her sake that weekend, Mudi told her that he had just been paid £600 as net for his previous week's work which included overtime. Within a matter of hours after going to bed late, M1 South asked for £600 from Mudi of which Mudi agreed and transferred it into her account that same day. Wow! Or really Mudi should say "No". Mudi agreed he would transfer that amount of money into M1 Sout's account that same day same day. M1 Sout then went into her bathroom for a bath only to come back crying, threw her face ontu Mudi's chest and sobbed like a baby saying the Holy Spirit had told her she (M1) was the one delaying her relationship with Mudi and that I Mudi was serious or genuine . Mudi then comforted her and asked her to write down in point form their future which they had discussed before- basically what they needed do cash wise: so she wrote a list like follows:

1. Mudi to look for a job in London and relocate to live in with her
2. Save money for marriage/wedding
3. Consolidate your debts (Mudi)
4. Consolidate my debts (M1 Sout)
5. Save money for Mudi's naturalisation and British passport, etc

But the as soon Mudi returned to Nuffinghi a few days later during the 2018 World Cup Football she rang Mudi round mid-week telling him a sick story of how she terminated her friendship relationship with a now ex friend a friend from whom she had borrowed £80 just because the friend had asked for their money, she (M1) said she was so upset about it because she believes that if she owes a friend or a partner some money they should not ask for it …. "sorry to remind you of last visit here last weekend when I fumed about you counting what you gave me, it's my principle that when I owe a friend or a partner money I borrowed from them they should not ask for it back and especially a partner they should not even mention what I may have borrowed or mention whatever amount they may have helped me with. Then she texted Mudi the last text Mudi ever got from her saying "I now aint have time for you… as I will need balance sorting out my debts, going to work, attending to my daughter (20plus year old), etc. so I aint got any more time for you"……☹

Mudi's response to the text was texting her saying the money he gave her out of love he leaves that between God and her, he does demand it back but as a human being the money she got from Mudi in the name of borrowing, Mudi expects her to give him back (£300 +£500 =£800) donate my clothes at your place to charity or bin them, wished her get luck with getting a hubby, partner or spouse millionaire or some man richer than Mudi as she had expressed before, saying a friend of hers and her own daughter had both once mentioned that she should get married to a husband millionaire.

☹ Typical undetected autism and personality disorder☹

Other weird behaviours displayed by M1 Sout.

1. Her dream house is a transparent lace house with "a real tree inside it"

2. Her then current house had no carpet nor floor boards nothing on the floors, it was all a bare cold cement floor including the stair way and the landing and her bedroom except bathroom maybe, wall some side wall paper removed and painted with white paint patches here and there. Her explanation for that state of affairs was that she had deliberately stripped her house as a strategy to make her daughter's then teenage friends and bailiffs stay away from her "uncomfy and poor" house.

3. All her curtains were transparent white lace material including those in her bedroom and she was adamant that her neighbours in the 2 or 3 story blocks adjacent to her bedroom cannot see her through her transparent curtains and windows which she preferred to keep open most of the time saying she needs her fresh air even in cold weather. She believed they would not have any time to peep into her bedroom as they were busy with their lives in spite of the fact that her bed was more than a metre high because she had 2 thick double mattresses on which she slept while her top back lay on what looked like a mountain of pillows and a back rest part of a sofa. Mudi ended up concluding that arguing with her was a waste of time and that this could also have been of result of her watching too much television programs like First Dates, True or A Lie, Wendy, etc and You tube video clips of different individuals from the reasonable to some of those people whose minds are among the most twisted or warped in the world.

4. She said she takes words very seriously and that the phrase "Good Morning" means "Good Mourning" hence she didn't want me to ever say Good Morning to her......in a similar vein although ironically and controversially, "her 2nd name literally meant "Trash", and she

said she wanted to change it to "Love", something she never did that time and she hadn't seen her dad for like more than a decade. Before exploiting Mudi at one point financially she had wept on the phone telling Mudi she couldn't cope with life in her fast, crowded cosmopolitan city to and wanted to return abroad and join her dad with whom she shared the second name which she abhored.

5. She also practised zero tolerance for any negative or sad story yet she said she would watched some horror films about which she said she would ask the Holy Spirit to teach and reveal stuff, revelations and lessons from the films. She saw things in black and white and seemed to struggle understanding "grey" or reading between the lines. Hence struggled with taking a "joke", unless she is the source and teller of the joke.

6. She said she raised her daughter in such a way that she could allow her go anywhere, mix with any type of people and she wouldn't fear for her at all even right from from the time she was as young as 5. She said at one point when she was still in primary school she went missing together with some of her peers and their mums drove to her door asking her to jump into their car and join the search for the young girls but she said with a boasting tone she refused to join them saying she wasn't perturbed because where she was she already taught her how to handle herself, therefore, she would still be back home. Up to this day M1 Sout's friends, after that incident those mothers, still do not understand M1's behaviour of indifference as she didn't have any intestines so to use an African to adage.

Mudi's final anaylsis of M1 Sout, is she seemed to experience a hotch potch of conditions which included undetected autism from childhood, fear of relapse of depression experienced in the past, fear of some individuals in

17

society abusing her personal information due to various motives which may include retribution to her for her meanness or abusiveness or other vices. In the middle of all such, she convinces herself that she has a very good personality. It seems apparent also that she tended to practice selective dementia in terms of what she wielded from different men of God even those 3 or whose teachings she claimed to follow – one of them Mudi recalled teaching "Never abuse any relationship" a statement of which M1 South tore apart left, right and centre with punity like she never heard it being taught. She had a serious subtle spirit of control and which the Bible says is like the spirit of witchcraft.….I had to sign myself off Facebook after she complained about curvy women she said saw on Mudi's page - individuals who were not necessarily Mudi's girlfriends, but simply curvy-curvy women. She then, like her previous tendency after pressurising Mudi to do something, "You didn't have to do that, you know"☹! She lacked respect for man, which is important and adequately she struggled to reciprocate love, she took a man's love for granted and that the man seemed to hold the view that a Man owes the woman everything while the woman owes the man muffing, absolutely 'nuffing, nuffing' and she quoted some of the late Dr Munroe's words out of context and for her own purposes, for example, she'd beat all the day light out of any man whom she would perceive as genuinely wanting to have her for keeps for the rest of his life – she would exploit, abuse and scam such a one, especially financially. A man who couldn't meet ALL her needs is not ready for a relationship and should not enter a relationship until he s ready" …she would quote such words to Mudi who she was already milking to the born…….. making Mudi feel very inadequate and wish he could rob a bank for her in spite of his already doing his best to the extent that by dedicating himself to providing M1

Sout's financial requests and Mudi was threatened with repossession of his flat by Council his landlord.

For almost 3 months Mudi had no choice but to be on the dole while he looked for a job(s) and ironically enough when M1 Sout used to be on the dole that's the stage when she had accepted Mudi's proposal with a "Now then, that we will be starting a relationship with each other you will be the shoulder for me to learn on, can I borrow three hundred pounds?....." Until when she shook Mudi off and elbowed him out of her boat, Mudi always faithfully and increasingly cushioned her financially without asking for her bank statement or questioning where she was putting her own salary nor demanding to know exactly how much earned. Terrible. There is loads that Mudi could have said here but allow him pen it of here.

CHAPTER 3

I Know
Why
I Write
What I Write
What do I Write?
I write exactly What I Write
When I'm Hurt I Write because I'm in Pain
When Tickled I Write because I'm Happy
When in Love I write because I'm loved
When Lost I write because I'm confused
When on Track, I write because I'm secure
I Know Why I Write
http://orwell.ru/library/essays/wiw/english/e_wiw

It is my wish that a foreword of this book be written by the EFF Commander –in-Chief Julius "Juju" Selo Malema, whom I view as a living legend and one of the prominent revolutionaries of our time with whom also, I share the same the very same dream of a United States of Africa which the late president of Libya Colonel Gaddafi was also looking forward to be become a reality one day. So, like Mark Antony in William Shakespeare's play "Julius Caesar", if space and time could allow me I would have wanted to wrap up all the 10 facts about the "good deeds of Gaddafi" listed below, with the same articulation with Antony expressed

his points about Julius Caesar to the shame of Marcus Brutus and his allies. Let me try . . . and here we go:

Friends, The Uxxxx Nxxxs, Nxxx, all fellowmen worldwide,
    lend me your ears;

I come to bury Col Gxxxxx, not to praise him.

The evil that men do lives after them;

The good is oft interred with their bones;

So let it be with Col Gxxxxx. The noble President Oxxxx and Nxxx

Have told you Col Gxxxxx was a dictator and abused his people:

If it were so, it was a grievous fault,

And grievously hath Col Gxxxx answered it.

Here, under leave of President Oxxxx and the rest

For President Oxxxx is an honourable man;

So are they all, all honourable men–

Come I to speak in Col Gxxxxx's funeral.

He was Africa's friend, faithful and just his people:

But President Oxxxx says he was a dictator;

And President Oxxxx is an honourable man.….

He hath brought many captives home to Tripoli

Whose ransoms did the general coffers fill?

Did this in Col Gxxxxxx seem oppresive?

When that the poor have cried, Col. Gxxxx hath wept:

Dictatorship should be made of sterner stuff:

Yet President Oxxxxx says he was a dictator;

And President Oxxxxx is an honourable man.

……………..

I speak not to disprove what President Oxxxxx spoke,

But here I am to speak what I do know.

You all did love him once, not without cause:

What cause withholds you then, to mourn for him?

O judgment! thou art fled to brutish beasts,

And men have lost their reason. Bear with me;

My heart is in the grave there with Col Gxxxxx,

And I must pause till it come back to me.

https://www.poetryfoundation.org/poems/56968/speech-friends-romans-countrymen-lend-me-your-ears

1. In Libya a home is considered a natural human right, is that dictatorship?

In Gaddafi's Green Book it states: "The house is a basic need of both the individual and the family, therefore it should not be owned by others". Gaddafi's Green Book is the formal leader's political philosophy, it was first published in 1975 and was intended reading for all Libyans even being included in the national curriculum.

2. Education and medical treatment were all free, is that dictatorship?

Under Gaddafi, Libya could boast one of the best healthcare services in the Middle East and Africa. Also if a Libyan citizen could not access the desired educational course or correct medical treatment in Libya they were funded to go abroad.

3. Gaddafi carried out the world's largest irrigation project, is that dictatorship?

The largest irrigation system in the world also known as the great manmade river was designed to make water readily available to all Libyan's across the entire country. It was funded by the Gaddafi government and it said that Gaddafi himself called it "the eighth wonder of the world".

4. It was free to start a farming business, is that dictatorship?

If any Libyan wanted to start a farm they were given a house, farm land and livestock and seeds all free of charge.

5. A bursary was given to mothers with newborn babies, is that dictatorship?

When a Libyan woman gave birth she was given 5000 (US dollars) for herself and the child.

6. Electricity was free, is that dictatorship?

Electricity was free in Libya meaning absolutely no electric bills!

7. Cheap petrol, is that dictatorship?

During Gaddafi's reign the price of petrol in Libya was as low as 0.14 (US dollars) per litre.

8. Gaddafi raised the level of education, is that dictatorship?

Before Gaddafi only 25% of Libyans were literate. This figure was brought up to 87% with 25% earning university degrees.

9. Libya had It's own state bank, is that dictatorship?

Libya had its own State bank, which provided loans to citizens at zero percent interest by law and they had no external debt.

10. The West Planned it all, is that dictatorship?

There is a clear growing conspiracy theory and belief that America planned all these, now Africans are starting to believe this.

Bonus: The gold dinar, **is that dictatorship?**

Before the fall of Tripoli and his untimely demise, Gaddafi was trying to introduce a single African currency linked to gold. Following in the foot steps of the late great pioneer Marcus Garvey who first coined the term "United States of Africa". Gaddafi wanted to introduce and only trade in the African gold Dinar – a move which would have thrown the world economy into chaos.

The Dinar was widely opposed by the 'elite' of today's society and who could blame them. African nations would have finally had the power to bring itself out of debt and poverty and only trade in this precious commodity. They would have been able to finally say 'no' to external exploitation and charge whatever they felt suitable for precious resources. It has been said that the gold Dinar was the real reason for the NATO led rebellion, in a bid to oust the outspoken leader.

So, was Muammar Gaddafi a Terrorist or a dictatorship?

Few can answer this question fairly, but if anyone can, it's a Libyan citizen who has lived under his reign? Whatever the case, it seems rather apparent that he did some positive things for his country despite the infamous notoriety surrounding his name. And that's something you should try to remember when judging in future.

Courtesy of Africa Cradle (2018) 10 Good Things about Gaddafi the don't want you to know Available at: http://www.africacradle.com/

top-10-good-things-about-gaddafi-they-dont-want-you-to-know/ Accessed on: 29/10/2018

Shakespeare W. (1599) *The Tragedy of Julius Caesar* Available at:

http://www.africacradle.com/top-10-good-things-about-gaddafi-they-dont-want-you-to-know/ Accessed on: 29/10/2018

CHAPTER 4

AFRICA UNITE!

Mudi thinks the event which precipitated the crisis, if not the jinx behind the disunity

Of Africa was the Berlin Conference of 1884 which divided and parceled up Africa into over 50 portions shared between major imperialist nations of the day. At that probably a few people expected this then seemingly necessary "development development" in the cradle of civilization, Mother Africa to lead to what appears like a permanent set up of Africa for the perpetual empowerment her foes, unending wars and woes like poverty, ignorance and disease. However, the combination of circumstances both in Europe and Africa at that time in history were such that this seemingly necessary "development development" (The Partition of Africa) set in motion a seemingly endless series of events which have plunged Africa deeper into what appears like a quagmire of chaos even up to this day. But now is the and today is the day for Africa's true sons of the soil to arise, turn round tables, recover all they lost and regain their glory as the dazzlingly shining Jewel of the world.

Africa Woye! Remember "Divided We Fall but United We Stand"! Viva Africa! Aluta Continua until We Complete the Revolution and make Our Dream Come True. Yes, Together We Can!

A Sickening Experience

Mudi and a female friend of his of Carribean background went out for breakfast in a local pubs first floor facing to the Old Market Square which serves some good breakfast before noon. Being a weekend the place was quite busy. Mudi spotted a free table No 107 which apparently needed the waiters to clear up the litter left by the previous customers. Mudi paid for the breakfast for two and when the waiter asked for the table number Mudi pointed at the table which was a few metres away and said "Number 107, but it needs cleaning please" The waiter said, "Thats alright, no problem someone will clean it up in a moment." In no time the table was cleaned. At the table next to the table which Mudi had just booked sat two young guys whom Mudi discovered afterwards were in a love relationship. For a better understanding of what transpired afterwards, allow me at this point in time to mention that the young man was black and the young woman was white.

Before Mudi could walk to sit at my table (the one which Mudi had booked), two white ladies who looked like sisters and had just entered the venue walked straight to the table and sat themselves down. So, Mudi turned his eyes to the waiter at the till and to his friend, the waiter told Mudi o simply inform them that he had already booked the table and was expecting his food there any time thereafter. Mudi then politely informed the two ladies two then only looked at each other but did not move. So, Mudi not wanting any confrontation walked back to his friend and he waiter and he asked the waiter to confirm the situation to the ladies and ask them to leave but then the waiter simply said "remind them that you are expecting your food there any moment".

Mudi walked back to that table and as soon as he said "Excuse me…." trying to politely clarify the situation to them, the black guy who was sitting at the next table having breakfast with his white girlfriend tripped, "Don't bully those ladies, man let decide what they want to order man". Mudi calmly responded by saying "I have already booked the table, and I am expecting me and my friend's food on this table any minute now, can find another table and book, please". Still they didn't move but resumed their chat with other and to Mudi's shock the black guy with a white girlfriend looked at Mudi who was standing quietly there thinking if he gave them a minute or two to decide they may understand and decide to move . "This is why I hate Africans", the guy said. "You like bullying other people. You were supposed to put a bag, a top or something at that table in advance to show that you want to book the table". Mudi replied, "Excuse me, I haven't bullied anyone here, I have only politely informed the two ladies that I have already booked the table and am expecting food for me and my friend who joined me just after I had ordered the food".

"I hate you Africans, you are just after starting trouble and bullying everyone… and you smell. I don't want anything to do with Africans". Mudi nearly popped his eyes out at a black man, ironically double darker than him talking like a racist to him and the guy's white girlfriend went "Yeah, Africans, they not only smell but they stink". Mudi just shook his head and said, "You sound sad. I know who are trying to please". Mudi's friend the joined the conversation "Why don't you mind your own business and leave him alone. How dare you two called him a bully and that he stinks? Do know what bullying is, bullying is what you are doing because I heard him speak politely to those two ladies and you just made up your biased assumptions and insulted him".

"He must be the one who puts on the nickkers in your relationship" he told Mudi's girl Jamaican friend.

"In your relationship, you don't only wear them you eat them nickkers" Mudi's friend chipped.

Mudi looked at the guy and said "I am ashamed of you, it's like you are insulting yourself. I know who you are trying to please but its only one day when your master spits at your face that's the day you will start looking for you father. You should go back to school. I'm actually writing a book about people like you, you know".

Mudi couldn't understand where that guy who looked and sounded Carribean, but then his mind was taken to a certain Jamaican who worked at a certain institution where he was apparently at that point in time like a decade before had done some voluntary work and when he asked for bus fare back home she gave him a long lecture on how her ancestors had worked very hard in that European society and made benefits that were not there before to be established. She had gone on say that Africans were now coming to have it on "a plate". Mudi got the bus fare from her, but as he walked down to the bus station that woman's voice had kept on sounding in his inner ear and as he pondered those words, a few metres close from the bus stop Mudi made a sudden u-turn, went back to that woman's office and her back the bus fare to the penny saying, "take this beck please, I dint think I need it, my programme has changed". Mudi only said it that way because e didn't want a confrontation with the lady who looked maybe 10 years older than him.

Mudi and his girlfriend's food then arrived at the table soon after the two white ladies had left and Mudi 's girlfriend showed Mudi an college topic she was working on. It was about "The Snow flake generation" and she started explaining what she understood about the topic and through the corner of their eyes Mudi and his girlfriend could see the nasty guy and his nasty girlfriend eves dropping an eye and in the meanwhile trying to eat their breakfast which had obviously gone cold by that time because of poking their nose into matters none of their business. They the left without even finishing their breakfast maybe because of the fact that it had gone cold.

After they left Mudi's Jamaican then explained to Mudi that that nasty guy was not Jamaican because his accent was not Jamaican and what he spoke was not proper Patwa. She said suspected that he was probably was from one Carribean island which had a history of mourning over the end of slave trade – those who wished the evil had continued, hence didn't celebrate its end and rather preferred to continue serving their masters. She said she wasn't too sure whether that was Monserrate?? or Barbados?? When Mudi googled the subject the closest articles he came across were The Barbados Slave Code (https://historyplex.com/purpose-significance-of-barbados-slave-code-of1661) and Exploration of Imperialism (https://www.reference.com/history/explore/exploration-imperialism).

When Mudi got to his house the more he pondered about the day's experience at the breakfast venue in the city centre, the more he felt his heart bleed for what he viewed as a "Lost generation of his people" who spit at themselves and always striving to run away and completely detach themselves from their very own shadows. Mudi found the syndrome sickening.

The pertinent question is: "Until when? Until when will an individual continue running away from his/her own shadow?"

Shame.

CHAPTER 5

CUT YOUR LOSES AND RUN

A few weeks Mudi's love relationship with M1Sout ended, that is, just before she had "borrowed" the last £600 from Mudi after a series of unreasonable financial requests she had made to Mudi and had been granted, Mudi, feeling vexed by M1 South's behavior and his head spinning thought of jumping onto the bus to town to just do some light window shopping to help him unwind, relax and distract himself from all that stress bumped into a stranger he will never forget at the bus stop.

A tall slightly slim lady who likes of mixed race but later revealed she was a light skinned Black British of Afro Caribbean background – born and bred in England though. She was sitting on the bench at the bus stop and when their eyes met her face lit up and did a quarter-to-three simile which looked way far genuine a smile than what Mudi once termed as "A Perhaps" (neither a smile nor a frown) in the book *Memoirs of Innocence & Experience* . Mudi reciprocally smiled at the lady as they greeted each other.

"Are you going to work?" she asked. "No, just nipping into town for a little window shopping and take breather, what about you?" " Oh, I am off to town to sort out one or two things but not in a hurry" she said.

" For how have you lived here" I asked. "Oh, it's like two decades now since I bought my house on this road" she said before asking Mudi, "Do you live in this location, I seeing you for the first time?"

"No but yes, I live in Clifching but at the moment I am temporarily y staying with my uncle along this road" Mudi

"Since it looks like we are both not in any hurry, can I invite you for a cuppa or coffee at my usual pub in St Jones street, if you don't mind?" she proposed.

"Oh, thank you , that's kind of you. No problem I can join you" said Mudi.

Mudi got this feeling of being liked by a stranger whose company felt quite warm and therapeutic. So, Mudi felt free to disclose the problem which was eating his mind to her. She listened very carefully to Mudi's brief account of his relationship with M1 Sout. Then she looked at Mudi squarely in the eyes, her eyes struggling to hold a few tears back, shook her head and said, "Cut your loses and run". Mudi stared at her without saying a word. "You seem not to have got it, do you know what that means? " she said. "But , the problem is I love with all my heart and I cant afford to be without her. Maybe she will change later" Mudi said. " You definitely didn't understand what I said, 'after cutting your loses what are you suppose to do 'RUN'! underline the word RUN. I know I'm a stranger to you but basing on the information you have shared with me, you are better off without her. Cut your losses and RUN, RUN, RUN away from her"

Mudi and his new friend-stranger had a some drinks at the pub and they parted ways. She refused to reveal to Mudi her address on the same street that they lived.

Mudi only remembered the lady's advice after M1 Sout had milked him off the last amount of £600 on top of the thousands of pounds which Mudi had given her before following either M1 Sout's requests or borrowing. 'Borrowing' had been one of M1 Sout's subtle magic phrases or overdrive gear to suck out extra money from Mudi.

M1 Sout. An evil schemer she was to Mudi. Mudi one of his friends that he has stopped getting alarmed by some stories of how some lovers made their nasty ex lovers pay for their "evil treatment" of them but he maintained that "Jehovah Gomollah vindicator as well as his portion"

"Blessed are the meek, for they will inherit the earth. Blessed are the meek, for they will inherit the earth" **Matthew 5v5**

Shalom shalom

Poem
Cut your costs and run

Two days ago

Mudi bumped into a stranger

The very morning after

His dream girl or dream spouse

Had told him to go

Find someone else nearer

The stranger asked Mudi out for a drink

AsMudi felt legless and armless

Following his sacrifice to M1Sout his then girlfriend

The stranger sternly warned Mudi afterwards

CUT your COSTS and RUN

Alas! Mudi's love for M1 Sout had then

Arrested His medulla oblongata,deafened,

Blinded and besieged Him to Hear No Evil,

See No Evil and Speak No evil

His then African Queen & Girl of his dreams

But reflecting his encounter with the stranger

Mudi rememberedthe saying

"We meet some people for a lesson & others for a reason"

And of course the biblical verse that

Some people have met Angels unaware

"Do not neglect to show hospitality to strangers, for by so doing some
people have entertained angels without knowing it". (Heb 13:2)

CHAPTER 6

THE WAYWARD INBREDS

Mudi says:

Just like the Psalmist in the Holy Book said
Even though everyone was conceived in inquity
All due to the ancient Adamic tragedy,
Some adolescents' upbringing exacerbatestheir innate state
Due to the bad parenting hereby their badness is irrigated,
Cultivated , cherished, treasured and rewarded
By way of animal –rights-turned human rights
That summarizes grossly rotten story of some societies
Any wonder why they swear, kick huff and puff at adults
At any slightest effort to teach them anything,
To correct and straighten their warped manners
"Shut Up!" they shout at adults even
To those old enough to be their parents or grand parents
"Im talking!" they have the cheek to shout when an adult
Asks them to pay attention and listen
Scoundrels and borderline rogues, maggots or
Dressed chickens without heads, good for nothing but gobbling,
Trumping and defacating – Goblins of first class order

Classic blinking idiots who resemble pregnant gold fish

Half wits who hide their heads in the sand like the ostrich

You catch them red-handed or pants down doing

Engrossed in some stupid … tupit act

And you ask them what the heck are they doing?

They stare at you in the eye and 'rudaftly' ask, "Me?"

"Yes you, of course!" you remind them of what they're doing

"No, I haven't done nuffing… It's no me.. I haven't done it!"

You ask them , "How can you deny such a clear thing,

I have seen you texting on your mobile phone

And you are even still texting right now!"

"You know the rules, holding or even turning you on mobile phone

During a lesson is not allowed" You say.

The little bxxxxx then quickly puts the gadget in between their legs

And blows their top at you

"Shut up! You are a liar. What are you lying through your teeth for?

I can get you sacked for that!"

The little bxxxxx shouts storming out with their phone in their hand.

And Mudi, steps back and throws his hands into the air, flabbergasted.

Wha…What……W-H-A-T-E-V-E-R

Mudi can't be seen to be arguing with a half wit, an

inbred, a fool, an imbecile or a whatever

Otherwise people will not tell the difference

In the background Mudi can hear some stupid,

foolish twisted rapping lyrics getting frenzy

"I wish someone rapped his or her school subject

content facts!" Mudiwispers to himself

"They scorn and abuse school staff and the

abundant resources at their disposal:

Build more jails for them then because such individuals
aren't aspiring to amount to anything in life
And ironically they claim to know more than their
teachers, their parents and their elders ☹
Blessed are those who succeed or who make it in life
through the dark tunnel or permissive system.
Simply implement the institution's behavioural policy
Full stop or Period

Food for thought

"God grant me the serenity to accept the things I cannot change, the courage to change the things I can, and the wisdom to know the difference"**Reinhold Niebuhr**

Read more at: https://www.brainyquote.com/quotes/reinhold_niebuhr_10088

CHAPTER 7

MATTERS OF THE HEART

I wonder why milk from a cow of whatever colour is always white
And basically the blood from whatever creature is always red
I wonder why the wind is never seen, yet we can feel and see its effects
On us and many creatures, creation, objects
and the flora and fauna around us
Yes, the effect of both Love and the Wind can
be felt by both man and nature
No wonder why Maya Angelou said;
"People may not remember what you did or what you said,
but they will always remember how you made them feel"
Love is a doing word, more powerful than feelings and death
What profound words these are!
But alas! I know several if not many individuals who preach
The words yet live the contrary, being the worst abusers
Responsible for the bad feelings, pain, wounds and scars
Experienced by their victims
They say don't do as I do but do as I say
Their Social media profile can read:
"Scatter kindness like confetti"
And yet they themselves are as mean as a fat cat

And as stingy as Shylockin Shakespeare's Merchant of Venice

If they ever part with anything "huge profit" must be the return

They love receiving and they lack gratitude

Yet ironically they love lecturing to others to give

Abundantly , generously without expecting any return

It's their God-given right to be receiving always and never give

Mudi warns such individuals to beware of the Dead Sea syndrome

Of which deadness resulted from "Ever receiving without giving out"

The only other form of giving they understand is to use others

T o give out on their behalf to those people they want to prove a point to

The point the love and spoiling they get can spill

over to their friends in the overflow

And when they do it they don't feel any pinch,

since the resources aren't theirs.

Sooner or later after that they ensure that they milk out their benefactor

At least a minimum of five times the value of what they have pressured their

benefactor

to part with towards their friends, children or kith and kin, that is if they

haven't fallen out with them

Their mentality is that if their benefactor can afford to spoil the above,

Then this means they have a lot more than what meets

the eye; so, like a merciless tropical tsetse fly

They suck use every "phrase", tool and trick under the sun to help them

suck their benefactor to death.

Greedy and bloody parasites such people are and the word *'Satisfied'* is non-

existent in their dictionary.

They belong to the fate of Dickens' character MissHavisham

of Satis House in Great Expectations

Because such people due to their selfishness can quickly

terminate their relationships with others

As soon as they feel they have nothing more to

benefit from associating with those people

Such individuals are experts at abuse, control and

exploitation of others before they drop them

Like the way one spews out chewing gum after they have

swallowed down all its sweetness and flavor ☹

https://www.litcharts.com/lit/great-expectations/symbols/satis-house

Food for thought

I wonder why most of us men many times deceive ourselves with the notion that we can ever meet all the needs of a woman's when in fact after God created them with everything good and beautiful they may ever need, then a lot of them shaved their eye brows and replaced them with pencil lines, they removed their eye lashes and replaced them with artificial ones, they shaved their hair and replaced it with either other peoples' hair, sisal or horse' pony tails and some went for facial plastic surgery, breast reduction, breast enlargement , bum enlargement and still yet others bum reduction☹

Philanthropy

Phila …. What?

Phila… a word which sterms from the Greek word Phileo Which means "Friendly love" Philanthropy means the love of humanity.

Philanthropy is a charitable giving to human causes on a large scale, undertaken byan individual organization based on a desire to improve human welfare.

However, the problem Mudi perceives is the fact that Philanthropy isone of the words very much abused by many people especially those members of society who are too ambitious, pompous, fame and power loving. Many a time some politicians are easily caught up in that fallacy of not only thinking they are philanthropists but actually calling themselves such declaring the title on official forms whenever they are asked to state their occupation. Mudi noticed a lot of such attitudes both locally and abroad. However, the most pathetic scenarios has ever witnessed with regards to the problem is when every Tom, Jill, Jack and Harry enter that arena, claiming to be philanthropists simply because they have thrown a few coins into a street beggar's plate. It becomes even sickening and criminal when even the meanest , stingy villains join the game, so that they can gain prestige and respect from their friend s and those whom wish to impress through "talking big" and adding the word "philanthropist" next to their name.

https://www.bing.com/search?q=define+philathropy&form=EDGEAR&qs=PF&cvid=ff8f810bd00e4d03b88b966d1a0a23fe&cc=GB&setlang=en-US

CHAPTER 8

POEMS OF REMINISCENCE AND APPRECIATION

The Year of the Locust

Your d.o.b Sir?

What d'ya mean "D.o.b"?

Do I look like I'm high?

No, Your date of birth , Sir

Gimme the month, day and year, Sir

That's all I'm trying to get from you, Sir

Oh my days, why complicate tings, mann?

What me Grandma told me wen me

Was a child is all I know 'bout it

The year of the locusts, seen?

'T was also on a night it rained cats 'n dogs, seen

She told me to allw-aayz remember

Lugubrious was the day and as such was the hour

Just before me was a born

Because all hope had waned

After midwife Granny Nadi had done

Evryting she knew 'n failed

So it was such hilarious 'n jubilant moment

Wen me said bye to me mum's womb

And made me first cry

With me both palms clenched tight

Jealously guarding me unique gifting

Which were still yet to be shown to the world

Me was to become perhaps a **Gy-ne-co-lo-gist,**

An En-gi-neer, an Acc-ou-tant, a Professor,

Or Whatever a role I and I was predestinated for

Wa-aaay before the beginning of time, seen?

In't this reminiscent of Jaques' in

Shakespeare'splay*As You Like It*

Act II Scene VII that:

All the world's a stage,

And all the men and women merely players;

They have their exits and their entrances,

And one man in his time plays many parts,

https://www.poemhunter.com/poem/antony-and-cleopatra-act

-ii-scene-ii-the-barge-she-sat-in-like-a-burnish-d-throne/#content

https://www.bing.com/images/

search?q=getty+immages+pumpkins&id=ACA8D

2CFCAB8C443F2DC80B32B14B416D5C99909&FORM=IQFRBA

Manhanga/Pumpkins/Calabaza

Malowe, Malowe, Ma-lo-we-ee

Manhanga in Chishona, my mother tongue

Iphuzi in Zulu, my neighbours' tongue

Malenge in Kiswahili Pumpkins in English

And Calabaza in Spanish

Come in different shapes

They come like pears, like oranges,

Like paw-paws, like apples, like onions

And still yet others come like tear drops

However, just like stars which are invisible

During the day or like the way the kahunas

Of a fly are, they are some that are like

the opposite of such

These are like anthills or mountains

Unmistakable to see and recognize

These remind the beholder

Of mountains such as the Nyotas, the Nyanganis,

The Kilimanjaros, the Alps and Mount Everest

Which all cause me to involuntarily burst out

Singing the old spiritual hymn "NdinoshamiswaKwazvo"

Or in English "How Great Thou Art"

(For images mountain images visit:

https://www.bing.com/images/search?q=mountains&id=9D1E
93C698CA7D61A6EBC192F401411D414825C9&FORM=IARRTH)

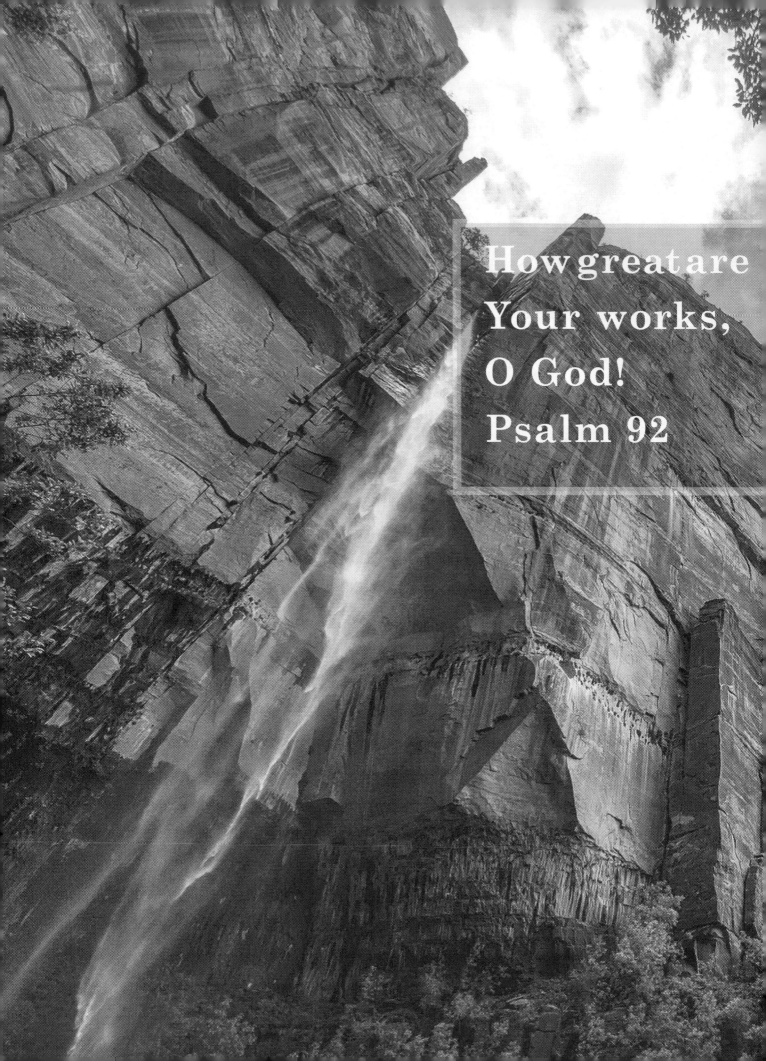

How great are
Your works,
O God!
Psalm 92

CHAPTER 9

IDENTITY

Until when, please just tell me
My brother, my sister, my child,
My nephew, my cousin, my aunt,
My uncle, granny, my grandpa
My friend, my in-law, my neighbor,
My Ex , until when my spouse
Tell me until Chomie
Will you continue to run away
From your very own shadow
When will you stop
Running away from yourself?
Forgeting the last person
To stick with you, is yourself
And your shadow
Why can't you be
Proud of your identity,
Your looks, your roots,
Your national or traditional attire
Your mother tongue
Or put simply your language,

And your good food;

I can see plenty of rice, chips ,

Fish fingers and mushy peas

And plenty fast foodsaround

The world today, but

Where is the sadza/tsima/ugari?

Where is the injera?

Where is the chapati

Where is the chakalaka?

Where is the yam and cassava?

Where is the ackee and salt fish?

Where is the egusi soup?

Where is the borshch?

Where is the boerewors?

And many more other dishes?

Yeah, why are you not proud

About the good things of your culture

The list can be very long

Don't you think it's high time

You started to take pride in yourself

Your hidden potential and capabilities

Who told to alter your lips

Through plastic surgery?

Or to straighten your beautiful kinky hair

Or to bleach your skin

Your roots are black but

I hear you say "I don't do black"

I don't do family, I do strangers

Non Uncles , non-aunts, non cousins ,

Or simply non –relatives

Well, it's your choice

But remember being extremist

In anything may have its pro and cons

I'm only concerned because although you are

Like pedigree black, I see you over

Smearing your face with foundation

Burying all the beauty of your natural tan

Which some pupils spend lots money to get

Something not as good but just close to it

With all that heavy make up you now look

Like Barbie, a commercial doll except for that

Plastic surgery on your lips which now

Look like they've been dipped in blood

Effect of the red red wine lipstick

My fresh concern now is, you scare children

And when you apply the pinkish and kakhish

Lipstick you look like you'vebeen eating anthill soil

Because I care, my advice to you is keep it close to natural

Otherwise, its sickening to me to imagine your influence to

Your off spring, as I see a man –made

Superficial extinction of the pedigree

As they get replaced by a type of a fickle hybrid

An caricature of a Snowflake generation

Alas, my heart does bleed concerning

The ways of a lost generation of some of my people

Reminiscent of a Hoto/Buzzard or the Alpine Swift bird

Very fickle and easily swerving to the will of the winds

Take a leaf from the Black Eagle, please, I plead.

POEM
Mountains

Like *pumpkins, manhanga, iphuzi, malengeorcalabaza* in Spanish

Mountains, *makomo or izintaba*come in different shapes and

Sizes sometimes like dynamites they come in small packages

Some of them more interesting to see than others:

Some are apple shaped, others pear shaped

Yet some more are square shaped

And others inverted or normal

Triangle-shaped, that is,

Top heavy versus bottom heavy

To say Mudi likes mounting mountains

Is probably indeed an understatement

Mudi enjoys climbing them, mountains,

The bulkier they are, the better for Mudi

Who remembers the biblical Caleb saying:

"Give me that mountain!" being confident that

he still possessed the same strength which he had

demonstrated forty years before he turned eighty five

Hence, Mudi also says like Caleb "Give me that mountain!"

No matter how much gargantuan it might beMudi would ask it

"Who art thou mountain before me?"and he would still climb it

Blessed mountains of both Africa my motherland and other

great Mountains of the world, in places far and wide apart, when

MudiBeholds our beauty, he stands still in amazement, mesmerized,

Tantalized and full of awe at the skillful hand of my maker who

created them all with unique and incomparable incomprehensible wisdom

par excellence, he usually finds himself singing "Then sings my soul,

my Saviour God to thee: How great thou art, how great thou art!"

CHAPTER 10

ADVICE TO LADIES AND GENTLEMEN IN LOVE

1. Speak to the king in your man and the king will appear and at the same time, speak to the fool in your man and a fool will appear.

2. Always remember how you make others feel will be remembered more than your words or actions

3. Do unto others as you would have them do to you. Avoid being a hard master or hard matron bent on fault finding at every turn and grilling and roasting others even for the very mistakes which you yourself does.

4. Man need a woman's respect more than they need her love. Give your man the benefit of the doubt and exercise good faith in them even after they have made a mistake

5. Never abuse your relationship with your man or even any other relationship you may have with your parents, your in-laws , your friends , your pastor, your subordinates at work, your boss and so on

6. Allow your spouse and others in general **to be themselves** - always remembering that you are not the model of a perfect human being and never try to reduce anyone's life to "a toy of your own imagination/dreams or puppet to serve your interests at the click of your finger and have them think and talk as you like

7. Suggest advice and in a good respectful manner bearing in mind that they are an entity with an independent free will and thay are free moral

agents- so avoid dictating and talking to them with a disrespectful tone of voice and if they choose not to take your advice on board do not get upset – if you do that's a sure sign that you have a controlling spirit which is associated with manipulation, intimidation, dictatorship and witchcraft. ALWAYS bear in mind that Advice is only advise and not a Command, a Bind and Fast rule or a Do or Die instruction

NB: ALWAYS know that advice is there to be either, Adopted, Adapted or Binned –no offence

In the same vein ALWAYS remember that there are many ways to kill a cat, so for example, To get a total sum of 6 any of the methods or sums present below are correct, so Do Not Roast Anyone over Your Personal Preference, for example being rigid that its only "3 +3 which gives us a 6" ☹**:**

3+3=6, 2+4+ 6, 1+5=6 , 0 +6 =6, 2=2+2=6 , 2x3=6 , 1x6=6

A Warped Society

The child is no longer just a child

And the parent no longer a parent

Since the State come in between the two

Hence leaving them all depleted of power

As a child my mum would clap me or even can me

Say, for having lost or misplaced my jacket at school

Or worse still if I ever swore at her

But today's parent just buys another jacket or jumper

Or simply advice the child not to swear

If a present day parent ever dares to slap the child

The child can call social services and the parent

May risk getting arrested or losing custody of the child

What a crazy society

Flooded with "Animal Rights" carefully labeled as Human Rights

Little is the system aware of that

Would it be alarming that sooner, the system may get

A rude awakening from the monster they have created ,

fed and moulded within the child when as they old pensioners they

experience the pinch if not the blow or nightmare of their own making

because they grossly spoilt their offspring by sparing the rod

Alas and behold, the fully grown monister which they

pampered and cherished, that inbred now runs amok

Like an elephant with a live ant inside its trunk

A system which sows wind often reaps a whirlwind

Gigo! Garbage in Garbage Out

That's just the way it is

Fare —ye- well

Asante sana, Good bye

CHAPTER 11

M1 SOUT

M1 Sout my Ex girlfriend
This poem I wrote
Soon after we parted ways
Four professions you
You know I have to my belt
One of them being a teacher
But to be honest too much
Love for you had blinded me
Regarding your character
To the extent that all I saw
Vividly were your positives
Virtues only, none of your flaws
Everyone told me, with you
It's either "Give me ALL
Of it or NONE of it at all"
That is concerning everything
I mean every good thing
I also realized that to you
"Mine is all yours as well
But yours is entirely yours"

Mine is only mine before I
Tell you that I have it
Otherwise thereafter
It's automatically yours
My foot!
Once I dared remind you
About such a state of affairs
That was it, my goose was cooked
I had to kneel and apologies
Profusely or else I lost you.
I also had to switch the mode
Of talking ONLY what's in your
Interest and interests you
Or else I was risking being ditched
And that's exactly what happened

Lessons Mudi drew from the above ended relationship

Real Love comes and flows naturally, it's simple and complicated

What you see is what you get, never imagine love where you can't see or feel it

Always check if there is "chemistry" between you and the one you think is your dream come true

If the clicking or the chemistry is absent, never fantasize about it ever sprouting, don't force or fake it

Because that makes the other naturally feel vulnerable and insecure, sensing that they are being used for convenience, just for a subtly planned season and only to be spewed out later.

There shouldn't be any pressure to put the better foot forward or fear to say the truth

because it is very true that Real Love Casts Away Fear

One needs not to rehearse nor first fast before saying something to their spouse

SOLUTION

STOP, Ponder/Meditate, like one playing a game whereby a Touch is a Move but in case you make a bad move quickly back off, re calculate your moves. Continuing after taking a wrong over is like knowing that route you have taken is heading the wrong direction then you keep driving, even if you cruise you wouldn't get to your destination.

Think deeply, cogitate and weigh all the Pros and Cons and be fully convinced Dude that your Love is like 150% for her and check also if she respects you like 150% and of course loves you too, although with man generally it seems respect is the thing most man require more than love if the two virtues were to put on a scale. The bottom line Midi thinks is don't waste your time tolerating a relationship with one who doesn't love you from the start: Love the one who loves you also

1984 forever?

Why is everyone having long noses?
Snapped an elderly dementia patient
When they asked her to confirm her name,
And date of birth at the theatre
One might be paranoid but never take it
for granted, they may ask you simple innocent questions
Whether verbally , in black and white or online
It might be a supermarket, departmental shop,
A hospital, a phone shop, a school, college, university,
Government offices, whatever institution
Aggressive marketing is on the rise
Far too many cold callers and yet Data
Protection preached like never before
For huge discounts in future
and updating about new products
And Special Sales dates provide your
Contact details please or visit www.xx. Com
And enter your details as requested
Every turn you make wherever you go
and at times even everyone you meet
Or interact with "a quest for Info, info"
It looks like the order of the day
Even at the bus card office, same story
Before you know it, they know more
about you than you know
This reminds me of a female friend
Who once said, "That doctor knows my

Body more than my husband does!"
Data collection, data collection
Some companies go an extra mile
By soliciting and collecting detailed data
About you from the data base and
Shameful to say, from some institutions
Which claim to subscribe to
The Data Protection Act
Other shameful realities are organizations
Or institutions which also claim to be
"Equal Opportunity Employers"
And yet diversity is in the ICU
When one scrutinizes their staffing,
Promotions, infra structures, Leadership hierarchy
Their protocols, operations and ethos
Then some institutions display this motto:
"Our core values are practice kindness, care and respect"
And yet in practical terms they act miles the opposite
Just as a case in point, Mudi once said:
The difference between a secondary school teacher and a nurse
Is while the former has the monopoly of teaching
His class his subject but the nurse doesn't have that monopoly
With his or her clients. The difference is like that between a lady
With one sole lover compared to a lady with a dozen or more lovers,
Or like a family on a prescribed diet with stipulated recipes and one cook
Compared to a situation whereby that same
family having a dozen or more cooks,
The inevitable in both of the second scenarios
is competition which unfortunately

Usually comes with friction and "holier than thou
or I can do it better than all" attitudes
And other selfish agendas like "snitching", "elbow
each other out" and "curry favouring
With the clients and their families" due to personal
insecurity wrapped in the fear to lose one's pin.
In teaching there is hardly room for any such drama, strive,
hypocrisy and tomfoolery of "working one's colleagues"
One word is enough to a wise man
A friend's slap is better than an enemy's kiss
The levels of hypocrisy Mudi has witnessed
In various organizations and institutions
Is sickening and anathema
Mudi abhors a "Perhaps" , a " Smifrow"
Or to make it plain a "Plastic smile"
As opposed to a "Quarter to Three smile"
Given a choice between Uncle Bob's frown
And Uncle Sam's " Perhaps" Mudi would
Be more comfortable with the former's frown
And agree with his post "Coup-Not-Coup" words
That some people are chameleons
Which includes Uncle Sam even as George Owen's
1984 seems to be here to stay
Written at 12:40 on 08/2/2018 and signed as Snow Black Mudi

CHAPTER 12

VARSITY OF NUFFIN'TING

Mudi says: 'Was' No, it' 'Were' it not for my good upbringing, good values, law abiding character and the concern of avoiding being labeled insane by society, he would have bxxxx dxxxx the blurry 150 sxxxx, cxxx varsity of Nuffin'ting similar to the way the late Marechera did to one local institution some decades ago. Right from its King Pxx's chamber down to the office of his most faithful lizard all because of the amount of racism, the pain, the tears, the stress and the unjustified delays it subjected me to during my studies at their self-overated racism dungeon. However, Mudi emphsised that because of what he went through he will not harm anybody, all he intends to do is take the institution to the cleaners. Mudi thinks it a fact indeed that for years on end they were overated until I read with gladness that their status was overtaken by that of another local varsity recently . As an institution, Mudi feels it's sad to say that the image of the few good individuals part and parcel of the organization if indirectly tarnished by those within the varsity who are as mean as fat cats, highly parochial minded, snobbish and proud of their faggy, faggy, maggottie, maggottie, disgusting tendencies of sweeping racism under the carpet letting students of ethnic minority experience unnecessary well calculated racist barriers meant to frustrate them and pressurize them to give up. Yet one hardly hears of any of their "Blue eyed boys" both from their home countries and here ever going through even a tenth of the discrimination, persecutions and struggles that their counterparts especially those of afro-carribean background experience. That institution, according to Mudi always looks drunk with its warped imperialistic and colonialistic tendendies of subjugating blacks, patronizing them as tools to serve their interests, including suppressing their fellow blacks' genuine complaints of racism in all its subtle forms , including institutional racism. That varsity is champion of Divide and Rule politics according Mudi's experience. At one point Mudi had a member of the Placement Learning Team who happened to be of Afro-Carribean background assigned to assist him follow up signing of his outcomes in one of his placement stations. This deliberately calculated intervention was done after 3 months of stress and sleepless nights. On a hot summer day, the lecturer to start with told Mudi to lean over and look at her computer screen for something she wanted to show him and she told Mudi that the problems of him not having been signed off were probably linked to the fact that he was smelling of body odour. Mudi who apparently as going through a lot of stress and sleepless night and had ruhed to her office for the signing off appointment was taken aback by this but because he already had too much to deal with he just told himself "This is one of the lost generation of my people". Afterwards when Mudi said he wanted to complain about the illtreatments he had suffered during the placement in question, she was quick to say "You can't change the world in one day can you? Concentrate on finishing your course, leave that to me . That's my job" That was it , , case diffused . She never did anything about until last a minute dog's meal work on it after Mudi had reported his case to OIA. Her hurried , last minute cover up efforts concluded the illtreatments and the delays which I had experienced on that ward during placement are quite common in busy wards .

Case twarted.

System 1 Student 0

Job Done.

She barked well for her bread.   Her master's divide and rule politics prevailed. Very true is the statement below;

"The master's tools cannot (if not 'can never') destroy the master's castle" Audre Lorde

Mudi feels they lack adequate support for black students and when they happen to offer it , it would usually quite late, a lot of damage would already have occurred to the students, psychologically, emotionally, etc and experience with them the time he was studying with them demonstrates that big time.

https://collectiveliberation.org/wp-content/uploads/2013/01/ Lorde_The_Masters_Tools.pdf

Expulsion and Reinstatement

Out of the 7 to 8 placement Mudi did during his training only three had good mentors. During his 2nd year 2nd placement he wrote a detailed reflective piece which was leaked an online news website (by someone whom he strongly must have been his ex girlfriend who had met the journalist twice without Mudi's knowledge) about an incident which Mudi felt was marred with glaring negligence and racism. He was expelled on 3 Sept 2012 after the uni had had just gone by the ex girlfirend's email whereby they begged the uni to expel Mudi.

The problem and the uni's weak or minimal and inconstant support towards Mudi dragged everything , subjecting Mudi to lots of stress. Instead of Mudi qualifying in Sept 2014 after starting in Sept 2011 at the age of 53 he qualified in July 2017 at the age of 56.

The uni wasted Mudi's 3' years and after all they admitted through their Fitness To practice panel that they couldn't find anything which impaired Mudi' fitness to practice.

When they s once took side with a mentor who had failed Mudi, saying he needed go for a stress assessment, Mudi wrote them saying that unless he got a letter of apology from the hc wouldn't atted the stress assessment appointment. He expressed to the uni that the stress was directly linked to the dragged and glaring lack of consistant support the uni had displayed. They wrote the letter and Mudi has a copy. That was not enough taking into account the tears , the sleepless nights , the stress, the humiliation, the expenses, the inconveniencing of plans and personal goals that the uni subjected Mudi to. This is just a tip of the ice berg there are a lot of gross misgovernance which that uni displayed. Mudi would never ever recommend that uni to any body especially anyone from the black community lest they experience what he was subjected to.

Mudi doesn't want to describe in details the whole case here because he has bulk information in the form of emails, letters, investigation documents of which time and space cannot allow here.

In any case the time for all that bulk evidence to serve its purpose is drawing nearer by each day.

NB: Mudi has feeling that there might many other individuals from ethnic minority who have undergone lots of ill treatments as a result of subtle racism and all its forms. Mudi would like to hear their stories and share ideas.

Send your stories and emails to: ichirawu@hotmail.co.uk

Below are some of the stories Mudi heard from other such individuals as above – (the names used below are not real)

Chiko

Chiko a family lady from a n African I won't mention here took like 5-6 year to complete her nurse training with a local university which name I wont mention here. Chiko kept on have problems of mentors and colleagues treated her withn attitude during placements. Mudi ended up seeing beyond the surface of things, it was nt hat Chiko was not good at her placement nor with her college work but it appears that the mere fact that Chiko had glaring traditional face marks which looked like wiskers caused some racist individuals to have a bad attitude towards her. The annoying thing is that they woud do the "perhaps" thing, thais a "plastic smile2 pretending to like he and yet failed her even where she deserved to pass. It took her almost double the duration of time which she could have taken to complete the course- all because of some individuals racist attitudes and her university which Mudi had studied had some individuals who swept racism under the carpet and not care to do adequate investigations

Tamari

Tamari aged 20 at the time of her studies , is a young girl from an African country I won't mention here . She was studying Radiography course at a uni somewhere up north of the UK. A whirlwind of racism cropped up and she got accused by some of her white mates for stealing one of them's credit card and using it to buy from a local shop. Tamari had no idea of what they were talking about but as usual a suspected thief would be expected by everyone to deny the allegations. So the accuser further connived with her allies no time reported the allegation to the police . Before the investigations started Tamari was told by her line manager that a patient had complained that when she she had fondled a client when she was assisting her change her clothes into wearing a X-Ray room garment. This allegations was also quickly reported to the police but her uni did not contact her. It was the placement comunnicatiing with the uni. The placement manager told her her uni had suspended her from that placement until she cleared the investigations….and a few days later she received the letter of suspension from uni.

The police took time to investigate both allegations. She was shown a CCTV video clip which caught a huge dude wearing a massive coat doing a transaction with a credit card in a shop. The accusers were adamant that that block was Tamari.

Tamari was called to uni and pressured to confess that she had committed both offences . She refused and told them that if they wanted to send her to jail for something she hadn't done she was ready to go rather than confess to something she hadn't done. They got upset by her response and told her because of "her rudeness" she was going to face a fitness to practice panel and in the meanwhile they wanted a DBS from the police. Mudi , Tamari and Tamari girl's parents fasted and prayed.

The police then told tamari they couldn't find any evidence or proof for both cases.

Tamari's trust of her uni warped and she applied for place at a different uni for her to complete her course

Vongai

Vongai ,a married lady aged 46 at the time . was studying mental health nursing at a uni in a neighbouring town to Mudi's. Vongai is generally an outspoken individual and very assertive in her undertakings. She told Mudi that one of her lecturers who happened to be her personal tutor Tracy   used to like her for her assertiveness nad at one point praised her in front of the class saying "People like Vongai, can easily be elevated to becoming managers soon after qualifying"

With time Vongai whose husband used to be violent with her , resumed his acts and so that affected Vongai's morale in class and it soon showed on her countenance that something was not right in her life. Instead of theat lecturer who once praised her , taking Vongai aside to find out why she had changed to becoming that much withdrawn, the lecturer picked on her and reidculed her in front of the class saying " You used to be very active in class Vongai? What has happened ? Is the course becoming more challenging now for you?" she asked . But Vongai was too stressed to talk , she just looked into her handouts.

When placement time came, a month into the placement Vongai was surprised to hear her mentor at placement saying "You personal has been here twice so far , but not wanting to see you. She has asked me to fail yo but from experience of working with you so far I can't see any reason to fail you".

It started to dawn to Vongai that her personal tutor Tracy was being unfair and biased towards her. Then she recalled that at one point during a lecture Tracy had confessed that her parents are racists and that she had grown being a racist but she wasn't any more. Later on as she continued with the lacement Tracy visited her and assessed her. Like the way veteran racists would do it, Tracy did not condemn every piece of Vongai's work but mentioned good things at the top of the report and then crucified her in the last paragraph saying that she finds no alternative but to fail. So, Vongai decided to report Tracy's attitude as well as get her account for her behaviour and the fact that she had previously visited the placement station and not seen her but had told her mentor to fail her.

When Vonage reported she was asked to proof beyond any reasonable doubt that racism was involved in Tracy's behavior and conclusions, in which case Vongai was asked to have her witnesses sign a statement confirming that Tracy had said she had grown up being a racist until she changed when she became an adult.

Vongai approached her several students in her class who were in the lecture when day when Tracy made that confession. All the white peers denied witnessing the incident and therefore refused to sign the statement for her. Vonage then approached two black girls from same country with her but according to Vongai because (1) the other white girls had refused to sign, they felt if they signed they would e victimized by the authorities and end up losing their course (2) because of the tribal politics back in their home country, the girls who came from a smaller tribe which felt suppressed by those of Vongai's tribe, they couldn't sign.

So, Vongai's efforts hit a had rock. Vongai felt exasperated that when uni told her because she had failed her placement and had failed her accusations about a member of staff's behavior and had failed to substantiate her claim she had leave the university.

Vongai ended up applying to a different uni in a neighbouring town and she started training afresh. At that second university Vongai failed some module when she was in 3 rd year and she failed to graduate. She then applied for a place to study a health and social degree course at a 3rd university. There she eventually made it and graduated with a BA (Hons) Health and Social studies

MUDI'S EXPERIENCE WITH UNIVERSITY of NUFFINTING

INTRODUCTION

MUDI (SO, THEN) APPLIED THROUGH UCAS TO STUDY MENTAL HEALTH NURSING (3 YEAR PROGRAM) AT UNIVERSITY OF NUFFINTING IN 2011 WHEN HE WAS DOING HIS MA IN EDUCATION PRACTICE DEGREE (1 YEAR FULL TIME) PROGRAM AT DE DIGMA UNIVERSITY IN LEICESTER, HARARE NORTH.

AFTER ATTENDING A GROUP INTERVIEW IN JULY 2011, MUDI WAS OFFERED THE PLACE TO STUDY THE MAIN DEGREE (BSc NURSING) PROGRAM AT THE UNIVERSITY OF NUFFINTING'S JANUARY 2012 INTAKE.

MUDI WANTING TO START SOON AFTER COMPLETING HIS MASTERS DEGREE IN SEPT 2011 ASKED THE UNIVERSITY OF NUFFINTING (UoN) TO SLOT HIM INTO THE SEPT INTAKE IF ANYBODY DECIDED TO DISEMBARK THE PROGRAM OR GIVE UP THEIR PLACE ON THE SEPT INTAKE.

AND, WALLA! TO MUDI'S DELIGHT & JUBILATION THE SLOT BECAME AVAILABLE & MUDI WAS CONTACTED & OFFERED THE PLACE WHICH HE GLADLY ACCEPTED... SO HE STARTED HIS NURSE TRAINING THE VERY WEEK WHEN HE WAS SUBMITTING HIS DISSERTATION TO DE DIGMA UNIVERSITY. AFTER SUBMITTING HIS DISSERTATION END OF HIS FIRST WEEK AT UNIVERSITY OF NUFFINTING, 2 MONTHS DOWN THE LINE, MUDI RECEIVED A LETTER FROM DE DIGMA UNIVERSITY CONFIRMING THAT HE HAD PASSED HIS MASTERS DEGREE AND WAS BEING INVITED TO ATTEND HIS GRADUATION IN ~~JANUARY~~ JANUARY 2012.

MUDI EXCITEDLY SHOWED HIS BSc NURSING PROGRAM LEADER THAT LETTER & TOGETHER

WITH HIS REQUEST FOR HIM TO BE PUT ONTO
THE POST GRADUATE 2 YEAR BSC NURSING
PROGRAMME OF THE UON. THE PROGRAM
LEADER TOLD HIM HE WOULD FIND OUT THE
PROSPECTS OF SUCH & GIVE HIM FEEDBACK
AS SOON AS POSSIBLE.

BANG! THE PROGRAM LEADER TOLD
MUDI AFTER A FORTNIGHT THAT THE UNI-
VERSITY'S POSTGRADUATE INTAKE GROUP
HAD SAID THEY HAD ALREADY COMPLETED ONE
MODULE & THEREFORE IT WAS TOO LATE FOR MUDI
TO JOIN THEM & THAT HE SHOULD CONTINUE
ON THE 3 YEAR PROGRAMME HE WAS ALREADY
DOING. BANG! ★※★☆★※★ SUBTLE RACISM!?
YOU THINK THIS WAS DISAPPOINTING OR A BLOW?
WAIT, YOU AINT SEEN NUFFIN YET. WAS THE
MESSAGE CLEARLY WRITTEN ON THE WALL?
THE VERY FOLLOWING MONTH MUDI WAS DEPLOYED
TO HIS VERY FIRST PLACEMENT ON THE PROGRAM.
HERE, THE MENTOR HE WAS GIVEN WAS AN
ELDERLY NURSE 3 MONTHS AWAY FROM HER OLD AGE
RETIREMENT. FROM DAY 1 SHE STARTED MOURNING
"THIS IS A VERY BUSY WARD, YOUR LECTURERS KNOW THIS
IS A VERY BUSY WARD", AND THIS BECAME A CHORUS
OR SOMETHING LIKE "AN AUTOMATED MACHINE
RHETORIC EACH TIME MUDI WANTED ANY FORM HELP
PERTAINING TO HIS COLLEGE PAPERWORK AND ASSESSMENT
OF HIS LEARNING OUTCOMES USING HIS WRITTEN
REFLECTIVE PIECES. HOWEVER MUDI RELENTLESSLY
WORKED HARD KEEPING ALL HIS GUIDANCE IN HIS
PLACEMENT LEARNING FILES

Mudi submitted to his mentor Mrs Whitcowe a dozen reflective pieces for assessment to help her sign off Mudi's outcomes set for the placement. To Mudi's disappointment & frustration Mrs Whitcowe sat on all of them only to give them back to him the day before the end of his placement with not a single outcome signed off. All what Mrs Whitcowe had done was dot some "i"s, cross some "t"s and reduced one of the reflective pieces to a version of its half its size and a comment that his reflective pieces should be that brief. This suggestion contradicted what Mudi had been taught at University & it wasn't consistent the Gibbs model of reflective piece writing. To more annoyance of Mudi, Mrs Whitcowe's handwriting was such a grotesque that could be equated to footprints of Jurassic creature on the sandy beach. Proper archaic, it looked indeed — comprising of some capital letters in the middle of several words which were supposed to be uniformly written in lower case or small letters, for example, "THE patient was given personal care." (sic).

Mudi couldn't help asking himself the question, "In which century did she do her primary school education?" And of course, "Did she use her birth certificate as her nursing qualification?"

As usually the case, where like the African proverb "THERE ARE NO WATERS WITHOUT A FROG", she was the frog in that unit! One good nurse who was mentoring another student, took Mudi into the office & asked him "How far with your mentor? Have your outcomes been signed?"

Mudi answered her "honestly" ~ "None at all"

"Oh I am not surprised, I have noticed that you have working very hard as a first year student on first placement but your mentor hasn't been supportive at all — right from day one". "Take a seat while I call your university's learning support department" she said with her eyes wet with tears she was struggling to keep back.

She rang the learning support department & spoke to a Vicky Furland & told her everything then she turned back to Mudi and said;

"Right Mudi. Vicky wants you & your mentor to see her at her office at 11am — let me call your mentor to inform her of this". She then rang Mrs Whitlowe before she turned to Mudi once more and said;

"Sadly enough Mudi I have spoken with your mentor has said she has got family tomorrow she cant attend that meeting with you so Mudi, just go see Vicky on your own tomorrow @ 11am"

So, the following day at 10:50 Mudi was waiting outside Vicky's office and, at 11 o'clock sharp, he knocked on Vicky's door. "Come in please" Vicky announced & Mudi opened the door & went in. "Yes, Mudi I presume" said Vicky. "Yes, I'm Mudi" responded Mudi. Then Vicky asked Mudi to hand to her his placement file which he was carrying. Vicky browsed through the file looking at each reflective piece & each piece of evidence carefully. "According to my opinion, as a first year student on first placement, you have shown enough evidence in your file to confirm that you have been working as hard as was expected of you — I see no reason whatsoever why your mentor has not signed you off all your level 1 outcomes."

Vicky then wrote four strong pages in support of Mudi and against the mentor (Vicky) and concluded by stating that Vicky has no alternative but to sign Mudi's level 1 outcomes — all of them!

When Mudi took that letter from Vicky to his mentor Mrs Whitcome, Mrs Whitcome read it by way of scanning through it & her face dropped but then she quickly tried to "debrief" herself by quickly spinning her chords & "this is a very busy ward" as she walked away from Mudi going to ask one of the patients some silly rhetoric questions typical of "hypocritical or pretentious questions" for example "it's a warm day today, you must be feeling warm today — isn't it?"

THEN AFTER SPEAKING TO SEVERAL RESIDENTS SHE
CAME BACK TO MUDI AND SAID " COME BACK NEXT
WEEK ON TUESDAY, I WANT THE MANAGER TO BE
PRESENT WHEN I 'SIGN YOU OFF YOUR OUTCOMES"
SO, MUDI LEFT THIS TIME RETURNING TO
HIS SECOND PLACEMENT ON A DIFFERENT
WARD IN THE SAME UNIVERSITY HOSPITAL.
NEEDLESS TO MENTION THAT MUDI HAD ASKED THE
UNIVERSITY'S PLACEMENT TEAM "NOT PLACE HIM
ON THE SAME HOSPITAL AGAIN FOR HIS 2ND OR
OTHER FUTURE PLACEMENTS" BUT NOBODY HAD
LISTENED. Another Subtle RACISM !

WHEN MUDI WENT BACK TO MEET MRS WHITLOWE AND
PRESUMABLY THE MANAGER THE APPOINTED TUESDAY
MRS WHITLOWE TOLD MUDI " THE MANAGER (MR
KAMAU) IS IN A MEETING — COME BACK NEXT
THURSDAY "

IN THE MEANWHILE WHEN ALL THIS DRAMA WAS
GOING ON MUDI'S COLLEAGUES HAD ALL BEEN
SIGNED OFF THEIR OUTCOMES FROM THEIR VARIOUS
PLACEMENT STATIONS & WERE NOW SETTLED IN THEIR
2ND PLACEMENT STATIONS. AT HIS 2ND PLACEMENT
(NON-BRANCH EXPERIENCE PLACEMENT) MUDI WAS
RECEIVED WITH AN ATTITUDE BY THE WARD MANAGERESS
A MRS CATMAN WHO EVEN PUT HIM ON A DUTY ROTA
WHICH INCLUDED SOME 50 HOUR WEEK ABOUT WHICH
WHEN MUDI COMPLAINED THAT THE UNI EXPECTED HIM
TO DO A MAXIMUM OF 37½ HOURS PER WEEK, SHE
RETORTED IN A DICTATING TONE " THIS IS THE WAY
IT IS HERE. NOONE WORKS ANY HALF-DAY SHIFTS HERE
PLUS I HAVE ENSURED THAT YOU WORK ON SAME

SHIFTS WITH YOUR MENTOR WHO IS ON TOMORROW." ~~LATER~~
AFTER ALL WHEN YOU QUALIFY YOU MAY WORK ON A
'WARD LIKE THIS!'" ~~MENTO~~

"MY FOOT!" MUDI THOUGHT ~~WITHIN~~ HIMSELF BUT DIDN'T
~~DARE~~ UTTER IT OUT "THIS IS A NON-BRANCH PLACEMENT."
COME THE NEXT DAY, AFTER A BRIEF CHAT WITH HIS
MENTOR MUDI REALISED THAT ~~THE~~ MRS CAT MEN'S
BOTH EXCUSES FOR ~~THE~~ DEFENDING THE DUTY ROTA SHE ~~HAD~~
MADE FOR MUDI WERE FALSE OR TO BE BLUNT "
& BLATANT LIES". Bang! "Subtle RACISM!
Again

THE 2ND PLACEMENT MENTOR ~~MS~~ Vangie Reynolds
& ORIGINALLY FROM THE PHILIPPINES ~~SHOWED~~ MUDI,
& ITER DUTY ROTA ~~AS~~ SHE ~~MENTION~~ INFORMED HIM
THAT ALMOST ALL, EXCEPT ~~ONE~~ OR TWO OF HER SHIFTS
WERE NIGHTS, BUT WAS TOO QUICK TO SAY "STILL
★IT DOESN'T MATTER MUDI, I WILL STILL SIGN
YOU OFF YOUR OUTCOMES, BECAUSE YOU WILL
BE WORKING WITH OTHER QUALIFIED & EXPERIENCED
STAFF INCLUDING MRS MEN AND AN ASSOCIATE
MENTOR. THE OTHER THING IS YOUR COLLEGE
~~YOUR~~ PAPERWORK COMES LAST ON THIS WARD,
ALL I WANT YOU TO DO IS "MASTER THE
ROUTINE OF THE WORK ON THIS WARD"
SHE THEN ATTACHED ME TO ~~SHORT~~ FEMALE
HCA OF PETIT-BUILT (WHO I REALISED

BEFORE THE END OF THAT FIRST WEEK (8)
OF "APPRENTICESHIP" UNDER HER THAT SHE WAS
ABUSED BY BEING OVERLOADED WITH EVEN HER
WHITE "COLLEAGUES' DUTIES, LIKE, I HEARD ONE OF
THE WHITE NURSES STAFF (KIRSTY) ON THE WARD SAYING;
"DESIREE WHEN YOU'RE DONE WITH THAT CLINICAL
WASTE YOU'RE TAKING TO THE SLUICE CAN YOU
GO TO THE THEATRE RECAN FOR BECKY BECAUSE
SHE IS SAYING SHE HAS BEEN THERE THIS
MORNING & SHE DOESN'T FEEL LIKE GOING BACK
THERE AGAIN TO PICK A PATIENT"
NOW DESIREE IS BLACK AND AFRO-CARRIBEAN
BY BACKGROUND BUT BECKY & KIRSTY ARE
BOTH WHITE.
IS IT ALARMING THAT MUDI BEING BLACK
WAS PUT UNDER WANGLE & DESIREE AS
A BLACK-TO BLACK STRATEGY - BANG *
Yet another Subtle RACISM!

The apprenticeship under Desiree was to last
One Week, AND FOR THE REST OF THE
FIVE WEEK PLACEMENT MUDI WAS
LEFT TO MAN A BAY OF SIX PATIENTS
WITH HIP-REPLACEMENT PROBLEMS ON
HIS OWN, DOING THE MANUAL HANDLING
USING THE OLD RATUNDA EQUIPMENT

..."COME BACK NEXT THURSDAY"... you remember MRS WHITCOWE HAD TOLD MUDI (PG) SO THAT SHE MAY SIGN OFF HIS OUTCOMES IN THE PRESENCE OF MR KAMAU THE MANAGER. MUDI WENT BACK TO MEET MRS WHITCOWE THE THURSDAY IN QUESTION. AS SOON AS MUDI PRESSED THE BELL AT MRS WHITCOWE'S WARD DOOR, TWO HCA (Health Care Assistants) CAME TO THE DOOR AND ONE OF THEM SAID TO MUDI, "MUDI, IF YOU'RE HERE FOR YOUR MENTOR MRS WHITCOWE SHE IS'NT HERE, SHE TOLD US TO INFORM YOU THAT SHE WORKED. LONG HOURS YESTERDAY AND SHE TOOK AN OFF TODAY — SHE WILL GIVE YOU A CALL AS SHE HAS YOUR CONTACT DETAILS SHE SAID"

Bang! Snubbed, yet another form
of RACISM!
SHE NEVER CALLED.

THEN MUDI FELT A LUMP OF ANGER, DISAPPOINTMENT & FRUSTRATION IN HIS THROAT AS THE AFRICAN PROVERB "A PRINCE IS A SLAVE ELSEWHERE" EXPLODED INTO FIRST AS A BULL BASS DRUM BEAT THEN AS A CHILLING EERIE DEAFENING CRESCEDO EVER

AS A WAY OF APPEAL MUDI SURRENDERED
THIS ~~UNUSUAL~~ SIGNING OFF OF OUTCOMES

"~~AREA~~"
TO HIS PERSONAL TUTOR WHO
INFORM(ED)HIM THE~~SE~~ SUPPOSED MENTOR
HIM WERE BEING "BRUSQUE" &
— DELIBERATELY FAILING TO
RECOGNISE HIM — TREATING
AS BAD AS IF ~~HE WAS~~ HE WASN'T THERE
YEAH AN ATTITUDE WHICH
~~DEMON~~STATES THAT MUDI'S
WA~~S~~ AY FAR Black to be NOT(ICED)
JUST LIKE THE~~M~~Y BECOME
OBLIVIONS OF SNOW AFTER
TRAMPLING ALL OVER IT
BIG TIME
AND IT TURNS BLACK, ARMED
& DANGEROUS, VENGEFUL
& PUNITIVE & SCHOOLING

"...TO IS TRAMPLERS & ABUSERS"
SILENTLY SCREAMING THE MESSAGE
BEWARE OF THE IDES OF MARCH
A SKELETON
IGNORE & TREAD @ YOUR OWN
PERIL

ITS BLACK ICE BLACK,
BLACK SNOW, BLACK ICE;
TIME TO TURN ROUND TABLES
AND HAVE THE LAST LONG LAUGH

YES, LOL BLACK ICE

THE GIANT SLAYER

CHANDO CHI TENACHI ORO PAGONO
BLACK ICE, THE DOMINATABLE,

JINX UPON THE MOUNTAIN
FOREVER TO STAY ON THE PINNACLE
OF THE HIGHEST MOUNTAIN

SMILE AT THE CLOUDS
THE FORMER SEEMINGLY OBSTRUCTORS
THE FORMER THREATING PHENOMENA
A CLOSE SHAVE TO FRUSTRATING
MY ASPIRATIONS, VISIONS & DREAMS
DUE TO THE CLOUDS' CEILING POISE

SMILE ABOVE THE CLOUDS
GLOAT & GLORY IN YOUR GLOSSY TRIUMPHS
FOREVER ON THE PEAK OF THE HIGHEST
GEOGRAPHICAL POINT OR MOUNTAIN EVER
BOTH IN MOTHER AFRICA & EVERYWHERE ELSE
...MT KILIMANJARO, MT EVEREST......
        BEHOLD)
ICE BLACK, YOU ARE MORE THAN BLACK ICE
YEAH I & I LION OF SNOW WHITE SNOW
I & I SNOW BLACK   ICE BLACK
        BLACK ICE
NOW KNOWING YOUR GULLIBILITY, ENEMY
OF MY DREAM, VISIONS, FREEDOM & SUCCESS
EPITOMISED & REPRESENTED BY A GOLDEN
GIANT GOLIATH OF OUR TIME & AGE,
-OUR ERA' AND DISPENSATION

YOU HAVE SWALLOWED IT
ALL HOOK, TWINE & SINKER
YET WHAT YOU SEE IS A MERE FACADE
A MERE TIP OF THE ICEBERG
ICEBERG NO, THAT'S HARDER THAN THAT
THE GLASSY, GLOSSY ICE YOU SEE
IS A MERE REFLECTION OF I & I
ME I & I IS DARKER & HARDER
            LO & BEHOLD
I & I IS THE PITCH BLACK PHENOMENON
YOU SEE BUT CAN'T SEE THROUGH
THE SEMI TRANSPARENT ICE
THAT DARK, HARD SOLID ROCK
YEAH THE DARK PITCH BLACK
TRIED & TESTED
DARK, PITCH BLACK SOLID HARD
GRANITE, GLOSSY ROCK
WHOSE ROOT & ORIGINS
CAN BE TRACED BACK TO ADAM
AND BACK TO THE TRUE ROCK OF AGES
THE ROCK OF ROCKS
THE ROCK OF AGES CLEFT FOR ME

FEELING A LUMP OF DISAPPOINTMENT
& FRUSTRATION & HIS BLOOD BOILING
WITHIN HIM MUDI DECIDED TO
SURRENDER THE SITUATION TO HIS
PERSONAL MENTOR, WHO THEN
SAID "LEAVE THIS TO ME" THEN AFTER
EXACTLY TWO MONTHS AN APPOINTMENT
DATE + TIME WERE FIXED FOR MUDI TO
MEET THE OLD MRS WHITCOME AGAIN.

MONDAY 2:00pm -
MUDI GOT THE 2.00 OClOCK SPOT ON.
MANAGER KIMAU SAID "MUDI, YOUR
MENTOR IS HIS HANDOVER WAIT, SHE
SHOULD BE HERE AT 2.20pm"
SO MUDI WAITED & SWEATY AT 2:00
MRS WHITCOME TURNED UP "OH, MUDI,
YOU'RE HERE WAIT FOR ME 10 MINUTES
I WILL BE WITH YOU"
THEN AT 2.30, SHE REAPPEARED
"OH MUDI CAN YOU GO WAIT FOR ME
IN THE HANDOVER ROOM, ITS EMPTY
NOW I WILL JOIN YOU IN A BIT"
MUDI WENT THERE & WAITED,
5, 10, 15, 20 MINUTES MRS WHITCOME

DID NOT TURN UP. 25, 30, 35 MINUTES
STILL MRS WHITLOWE WAS NOWHERE TO BE
SEEN, 40, 45 MINUTES, THEN SHE
APPEARED AT THE DOOR "OH I FORGOT
TO BRING THE MANAGER" THEN SHE
VANISHED AGAIN.... THEN AT 3:20
EXACTLY 50 MINUTES SINCE MUDI's
ARRIVAL FOR THE APPOINTMENT SHE RETURNED
STILL ALONE
   "OK NOW LETS SEE YOUR FILE AND SEE
    IF I CAN SIGN YOU OFF"
MUDI GAVE HER THE SAME OLD FILE
+ ITS PREVIOUS CONTENTS FROM THE TIME
HE FINISHED THE AGREEMENT (2 MONTHS
BEFORE)

Whats' all this dragging of feet on top of
all the prior SNUBBINGS
     Another form of subtle RACISM
hinged on "Stereotyping" - that if you
stretch a 'Blackman's patience' too far
"he will blow his top SWEAR + HUFF
   + PUFF AND WALK AWAY' as
in SULKING! Then she Mrs Cateowe

WOULD WIN, AND SAM:
"HE FAILED TO UNDERSTAND THE
DYNAMICS OF A BUSY WARD —HUFFED,
PUFFED, FUMED & SULKED GIVING
ME NO CHANCE TO SIGN OFF HIS OUTCOMES
DUE TO HIS ~~XXXX~~ IMPATIENCE
& SHORT TEMPERAMENT"

AND THEN IF THEIR AUDIENCE IS EQUALLY
"PREJUDICED RACIST ~~SNOBBISH~~
HIGHLY PAROCHIAL MINDED
AND SNOBBISH, THEY WOULD LOOK
AT EACH OTHER DUMP MUDI
WITH "AND HE WANTS TO BE A NURSE?
HE WOULDN'T GO FAR WITH IMPATIENCE
AND A HOT TEMPER, WOULD HE?

~~BANG~~ SUBTLER RACISM!

~~UPSTREAM~~ BUT THANK GOD, MUDI
"CONTINUED TO BE PATIENT & KEPT
HIS CALM. ~~THESE~~
THE SIGNING OF THE OUTCOMES THEN
STARTED @ 15:20 AND ENDED
AT 18:00hrs, with on small
booklet undone which she was
to do on her own & leave

at the manager's office for Mudi to collect the following day.

All the above drama was going on while Mudi was undergoing worse treatment on his 2nd placement

Due to the hardluck of managing a bay of six patients on his own using an old rotunda to move them from bed to chair & vice vesa, Mudi sustained a shoulder ~~strain~~ muscle sprain.

When Mudi tried to solve it by referring to the placement 1st then ask for permission to visit the A & E dept the associate mentor had her own jab of frustration.

"Mudi; "Excuse me," said Mudi requesting associate mentor's attention she ignored Mudi three times until before finally snapped

"Whatever it is, we will talk after handover"

"I'm ~~aint~~ feeling too well, I have to visit A & E" mumbled Mudi leaning himself against the wall struggling to stand upright, in pain

"YOU GO THEN!" SHE EXCLAIMED, ~~COLDLY~~ EMOTIONLESSLY LIKE AN ~~AUTOMATED~~ TALKING MACHINE

PAUSE A MINUTE, WHO WAS THIS SUPPOSED TO BE?

That's a youngish white woman probably half the age of Mudi & she is the appointed associate mentor for Mudi who was doing his 1st year Nurse Training Course's 2nd placement

~~Being~~ * subtle RACISM

IT WAS DURING THAT VERY SAME PLACEMENT WHEN MUDI HEARD THE VOICE OF BLACK MAN WHOM ACCORDING TO MUDI'S REFLECTION & DETAILS IN HIS WRITTEN REFLECTIVE PIECE WHICH ~~WAS~~ LEAKED TO AN ONLINE NEWS WEBSITE, WAS NEGLECTED AND AS PART OF THE,

UNIVERSITY & ITS HOSPITAL & THE SHXTSTEM'S (TO USE THE LATE P. TOSH'S "COINED WORD" COVER UP, MUDI WAS

EXPELLED!

BY suble RACISM!

'WHAT THEN HAPPENED AFTER THIS POINT IS A SERIES OF SICKENING EXPERIENCES WHICH MUDI WENT THROUGH, WAS SUBJECTED TO & SUFFERED IN THE HANDS OF THESE CARICATURES OF THE HIGHLY PAROCHIAL-MINDED, SNOBBISH & GROSSLY ARROGANT DESCENDANTS OF THE OLD "SLAVE MASTERS"

OUT OF 8 PLACEMENTS MUDI HAD ONLY 3 MENTORS WHO WERE UNDISCRIMINATORY & GENUINELY SUPPORTIVE TO HIM — THESE WERE ONE ZIMBABWEAN
ONE BRITISH
ONE IRISH

AND THERE WERE OUTSTANDING LECTURERS 1 British 1 Scottish

DETAILS REGARDING THE
EXPULSION & AFTERWARD
REINSTATEMENT ON CHEEKY
IF NOT CRUEL CONDITIONS
~~AFTER~~ COSTING MUDI
TO LOSE 3 YEARS OF
HIS TRAINING CAN BE
AVAILED TO GENUINE
GOOD SAMARITAN LAWYER
OF HUMAN RIGHTS WILLING
TO "CLEAN" THE DIRTY VARSITY
IN QUESTION.

(1) AMONG THE BAD LECTURERS WERE:
AFRO CARIBBEAN WHO BLOCKED
MUDI FROM MAKING FORMAL
COMPLAINT IN TIME AND HE
TOLD MUDI HAD "BAD BODY ODOUR"
(2) A ~~WHITE~~ BRITISH WHOSE NAME SOUNDS
LIKE TIA BOGLY WHO ENJOYED SEEING
MUDI'S TEARS
(3) BAD MENTORS

AMONG THE 4 BAD ONES, ONE (ANIMAL) FAILED
MUDI'S BANK PLANNED FINAL PLACEMENT
CHALLENGING ON 10th DAY OF 30 DAYS
"DO YOU THINK YOU CAN STAND SIDE BY SIDE WITH US?"

MVDI FEELS THE
SUBTLE FORMS
OF RACISM

range from
Individual/personal
Communal/Organisational
Institutional/National
Continental and even
right down to Global/
International or even
Universal

Some things seems to never
change
Maybe until the 2nd Coming
of the Lord of Peace + Righteousness

FOOD FOR THOUGHT

I AM SPLIT BETWEEN CALLING THE VARSITY IN QUESTION

"UNIVERSITY OF NUFFINGTING"

OR

"UNIVERSITY OF NUTTYTING"

, I THINK FOR A PSEUDONYM THE LATER IS MORE FITTING FOR THE FLIPPING INSTITUTION

For years they rated themselves as in TOP 10, my foot!

PAY BACK TIME: Only possible when The Swallow bird dares to realize that after all The Owl ain't got any horns or when the buffaloes realize that united they can defy the lions' fear striking and divide and rule strategies and school the lions big time – gorging them and sending them flying into the air and running helter skelter for dear life. Then and only then is the African proverb fulfilled that "the old hunter of all time memorial has now become the prey". In simpler language "The tables have been turned round" "What goes around comes around: he that sowed wind has now reaped the whirlwind – the chickens have come home to roost".

Aluta Continua! Victory is certain and together we can complete the Revolution! Africa Woye! Long Live Mother Africa, the cradle of Civilization! Icho-o charira – Fire! Boo-ooooom!!!

Without controversy the first shall be the last and the last shall be the first….. It's now Africa's Time.

Amen.

PS: Yippie, Mudi the Cushite has just discovered a mountainous area with lots of lakes somewhere in the north western direction of an island which lies North West of Africa and South West of the North Sea. He has decided to name the area Emperor Haile Selassie Lakes (selah).

There is nothing as exciting as being found ready when opportunity knocks at the door.

The same university which Mudi cartooned in the last part of my handwritten doc, previously discriminated the mother of his children in 2006 on health grounds, by dropping her off a nursing program she had embarked on only 2 or so months down the line after she had started. Their reason was "...we fear that you may not cope with placements, go and work on your weight" and yet she had passed their occupational health check just before she started. Mudi urged her to fight them but she refused, then the stress effect of that setback and 'discrimination on health grounds' exacerbated her obesity in the approx 3 years which followed, directly influenced and precipitated the crisis that led to Mudi's divorce, the process of which began in 2009. In that same year when his ex wife had started studying with the Varsity of Nuffighi or nuffingtin or is it Nuttyfing, Mudi graduated different local uni where he was inferringly called "a monkey" by a white girl and an elderly white female lecturer endorsed the insult – a flimsy apology was made after one of Mudi's friends (a female student of Afro-Carribeen background) grilled the lecturer the following day for the uncalled for behavior. After that when Mudi approached the Race Equality council seeking to make a formal complaint, the mixed race guy who ran the office was pathetic. To start with as he spoke rocking in his chair Mudi noticed his trousers was split between his legs and he wasn't wearing any underwear hence quite a glimpse of his testicles were exposed. After Mudi finished narrating his story, the guy laughed and said, "So, what do you expect to get from the uni except probably a mere apology and of what good would that be that to you?" What should I have done then? Mudi asked, to the guy's further amusement. "You should have called them something similar, just like they insulted you1" and he laughed his lungs out. Mudi's conclusion was the shxxstem knew who put in what position to twart black people's racial discrimination complaints – he was barking for his supper. What was supposed to be Mudi's last placement, didn't work out as young white lady his then mentor there, had quizzed him with many questions about his background only to use it against him afterwards, resented him for being a refugee and influenced other 2 teachers in the department to team up with her to change goal posts for him and she failed him 7 weeks before graduation. His link tutor observed him teach and with tears-filled eyes told Mudi, "I'm happy with your teaching but I don't know where your mentor is getting the bad things she is saying about you. I will get you another placement to finish your course". He managed after 5 months due to that Mudi missed his graduation that December and had to graduate the following July. Mudi got his PGCE with tears. That what the Shxxstem wanted. What a bag of maggots of a system it is! The problem resulted in Mudi going out with Vongai, now his ex who wrote a sick email to one of the uni's lecturers which the uni gullibly believed and expelled Mudi without making any investigations. Is this alarming in a shxxstem which practices selective dementia, tending to value animal life thatn some humans lives as Mudi recalls Vongai being granted asylum for claiming that her dog which was poisoned by burglars, was shot dead by uncle Bob's supporters – Vongai fully suppressed her typical Cushite belly laughter as she saw the shxxstem agent's eyes flooded with tears as he beheld a photo of the dead dog. Mudi cannot dismiss imagining "what would have happened" if that agent was one of his former lecturers or the "white bootlicking and slavery-perpetuation-loving black guy" (at the breakfast pub) who both called him he smells, just because he is African, forgetting that they two bear a stench as they are their "master' stools'" (whatever) who cannot destroy their master's castle" and bark for their supper.

Don't get Mudi wrong, he has got many progressive thinking, pan African friends of Afro-Carribbean background who have shared with him very constructive and inspiring words of advice especially with regards to "positive self-esteem and how to keep one's head above the murky waters of the shxxstem", among those good friends are Prince Bravo and Corporal Blaze (p130-131 Memoirs of Innocence & Experience). Mudi also has great respect for British writer, poet Benjamin Zephaniah whose political ideas and perceptions concerning the diaspora society I resonate with. Because of the stress, cost, lost of time and dehumanization, the risks/vulnerability and the further delays (whereby the uni continued to be prejudiced and scarcely supportive, dragging its feet like a snail) which all this caused to Mudi, Mudi at one point demanded £100k from the uni's vice chancellor. Ironically enough, have since seen some white staff at the same uni one and half times if not double the size of the mother of my children, since then. Mudi got his Diploma qualification with tears. That what the Shxxstem expected. What a bag of maggots of a system it is!

NB: Mudi couldn't be bothered typing the version narrating some of the ordeals he faced regarding placements and the uni's attitudes towards him, produced a handwritten account instead, as he awaits the ripeness of time to take the flipping uni to the cleaners since he has all the official written documents which includes letters and emails and others in bulk. Moreso, Mudi believes that "sorry is not enough to a lawyer" and a case doesn't rot like meat.

DZIDZAI FINAL

DZIDZAI, FUNDAI MUDZOKERE KUMUSHA

Chinono chinengwe, dindingwe rikadya richifamba
Ngatifundei, ngatidzidzei vana veDzimbahwe
Tisazofunga bako tanaiwa nemvura
Ngaticherei mwena, nguva ichwanikwa
Ngatidzidzei pamujuru nemashosve
Tupuka tunenge tusina mambo, tusina simba
Asi tuno shanda nesimba tuchiunganidza mbuva
Zuva nemwaka wenzara zvisati zvasvika
Mwana kana muranda anodyara hope muzhizha
Muchirimo anokohwa zhara nekudemba-demba
Zhizha redu ndinhasi, Chirimo chedu ndimangwana
Zhizha redu ndoKuno, Chirimo chedu kuMusha

Dai kamba dzaiwanikwa kuno
Pamwe taizoti charova sei chando
Chakwidza hamba mumuti
Zvino bva tototika charova sei chando
Chapfekedza squirrel magloves
Kana kuti chaomesa makungwa ose
Kunge padunhu kutendera ngorodzemoto
Kudhiriridza dzichibatanidza pasi rose
Zvikepe zvatova sezvuru nemakomo

Ngatiregei kanganwa kutambura, nezhara yazuro
Nokuda kwekuzvimbirwa kwanhasi hama dzangu
Unyangwe hazvo zvikanzi 'kare haagare ari kare'

Tirangarirewozve kutika, 'nhasi harambi ari nhasi'
Uye, 'nhoroondo inogona kuzvidzokorora pachayo'
Ko, kana vasina mabvi, masvetaropa, vakokorodzi
Vakagona kupamba nekurozva jahwi repfuma yedu
Goridhe, mhangura, madhamonzi nejakwatira razvo
Isu tinotadza neiko, kurozva, kukorokodza mongo,
uchi, munamba nehwadyehwerongo hwepfuma yavo.
Tinoziva vakashandisa penzura nepfuti vakateura ropa,
Zvinoka nhasi zvinonzi, anemari ndiye mukuru
Asi ndoti anenjere nokunzwisisa ndiye mukuru

PART TWO

Hama dzangu vadikani vana vevatema
Ngaticherei pakuru kubva munyanza uchenjeri
Zivo, Kunzwisisa nePfuma
Tozvitungamidza mberi saJacobho kuna Esau
Tidzosere makomborero edu ose kuMusha
Tirimubishi nemutsimba nevatongi
Tipiwe gwara tidzokere kwatakabva
Nokuti isu, tasuwa hama dzedu dzose
Dzakasara kunyikayo yerurukuvhute rwedu
Amai Afrika, Amai Mambokadzi Afrika
Dzinde reruvheneko, Amai veMunhu
Bindu rezvicherwa zvose zvinopundutsa,
Tsime reMukaka watakanwa wakatiyarutsa,
Chitubu chemvura yakapedza nyota yose
Pakati penyika pakatekeshera chiedza nezuva

PART THREE

In Vukulan one young lady complained to an elderly postman
About window envelope letters she received daily cause they were debt mail.

The oldman said, "I actually envy you. You're very fortunate to have someone trust you with a debt. I wish I got a $million plus debt then just die without paying it back. I wouldn't give a rut because at least I would have handled a $million in my life time and though dead I would have enjoyed myself. What would happen afterwards I would not be my worry or business at all? He dared say that even though in Vukulan the creditors would fight tooth and nail with the backing of the law attach all property or assets in the old man's name and auction it to recover the debt both while he is alive and even after he is deceased. But in Vuku North three is no such thing as the courts of law defending the creditors BIG TIME, they instead tend to side more with debtor. If the debtor reasonable enough to indicate a (willingness to pay) "the heart is willing but the pocket is weak" they may be asked to pay even as little as 1pound per week usually from their dole (Social fund handout/unemployment benefit) and those banks they owe thousands from credit cards, loans and overdrafts simply lose out and if the interests charged by the banks are judged as exorbitant the debts may be written off. Moreover the debtor also has a choice to declare themselves bankrupt and end up with no debt to pay at all. If the debt owed a 'loan shark' (illegal money lender), the courts of law would irrefutably let the debtor go scott free and advise them not pay back even a penny – no matter how much they owed. And this is bit, no matter how much noise the creditors may make about litigation, bad listing and no matter how many red letters they may send the debtor, the debtor would not be bothered anywhere about 'bad listing' when they are already in deep in debt because once more attachment of assets and property or imprisonment for unpaid debt(s) is of out of question in Vukulan North.

PART FOUR

Chakanakira Chirungu kuno
Havagure musoro wemukwereti asinga bhadhare
Kana kumutorera zvose nechisimba kusvikira patsono
Kana kumukanda mujere , kwete,
Ndosaka sekuru Panofamunhumashokoanowanda
Anongonzi "P" namakiwa kuno Vukulan North
Vakazotiwo, "Dai ndawana anondikweretesawo
Miriyoni yepondo, ndigozofa zvangu
ndisina kubhadhara kana kobiri. Hazvina mhosva
nokuti ndinenge ndamboibatawo Miriyoni
uye ndambonakirwa ndichiziva kwazvo kuti
chikwereti hachizoiswa pavana kana
pahama dzangu dzinenge dzasara"
Shuwa, kufa kwasekuru P ndikokufa chikwereti chafawo

Saka munyika yakadaio kudai, wakazofunga
NezvaRobin Hood gamba ravo muguta rino
Uchawona kuti wakaita sezvakaita vana veIsraeri
PaEjipita gore riya vasati vatama "vakarozva ma Ejipita"
Vakapiwa pfuma yose yavaida vakasaidzora
Nokuti vakaropafadzwa kuti zvidaro
Zvakatsivana ne uranda ne usarura hwaiitirwa kwemakore
Kana ukazoverenga buku remavambo 47v14 uchapa kutenda
Saka kokorodza pfuma kana ndarama yose kana uchigona
Kana kuti saRobin Hood, iwe bira vapfumi
(ivo vakabira varombo kare)
Ugopaka varombo, zvikuru sei vari Vukulan, zviringane.
From Vuku with only a rod and a staff and back

To Vuku – loaded like Jacob or Israel on his way from Laban
PS: Soko iri harisi rokutaura, nderekungoita
CHINYARARIRE!
Ndokungwara, Ndokuchenjera
Anenge ochenjedza vanyamukuta
Kuzvara achada ndiye mutengesika
Anovaviwa neshawe reurombo neuranda
Achirara nezamu mukanwa vamwe vachikohwa
Rangariraka kuti
Anogona kurwa chaiye haana nguva
yekupambadze namashoko mazhinji
Anongokinditsa, anongorakasha,
kuzhanda-zhanda kana kutonhodza
CHINYARARIRE!
The Vukulan North system is colder than its winters
And its such a cold system that makes one clearly see

That characters like the late Bin Laden, the late Colonel M. Gadaffi, Mudi's former president R.Mugabe and the rest of those perceived as enemies of the West are to an extent products of the system's confusing ice-cold fluidity-rigidity and politics of divide and rule of which the above entities and many others defied. Now, talking about racism on an International scale, one of the above politicians mentioned among other things that the representation of Africa in the UN Security Council is appalling and that the headquarters is geographically misplaced "centrality wise" and also in terms of statistics of the people from different races which that body must represent.

**ANOTHER BOOK WILL BE PUBLISHED
AS A SEQUEL TO THIS ONE.**

REFERENCES

Goalcast (2017) The Most Important Time of Your Life
Available at: https://www.goalcast.com/2017/02/28/the-most-important-time-of-your-life-martin-luther-king-jr Accessed on:15/11/2018

(Hondo) Chirawu, I B (2011) Memoirs of Innocence & Experience: Through the Eyes of a Village Boy
Available at: https://www.xlibris.com/bookstore/bookdetail.aspx?bookid=SKU-0301371003 Accessed on: 15/11/2018

Orwell, G (1946) Great Ideas Why I Write, Penquin Books Available at: https://www.amazon.co.uk/Penguin-Great-Ideas-Why-Write/dp/014101900X Accessed on 15/11/2018

Saunders, G (2017) The Guardian: What Writers Really Do When They Write Available at: https://www.theguardian.com/books/2017/mar/04/what-writers-really-do-when-they-write Accessed on: 15/11/2018

VOA Zimbabwe (2016) President Mugabe Showers Praise On UN Chief As He Rebukes Body's Lack Of Reform
Available at: https://www.youtube.com/watch?v=ql_EyB-bqOk Accessed on: 15/11/2018

Printed in the United States
By Bookmasters